Healers of the Wild

SECOND EDITION

Healers of the Wild

Rehabilitating Injured and Orphaned Wildlife

DONNA CLEMENT

Shannon K. Jacobs

Johnson Books
BOULDER

Published by Johnson Books, a division of Johnson Publishing Company,
1880 South 57th Court, Boulder, Colorado 80301.
Visit our website at JohnsonBooks.com.
E-mail: books@jpcolorado.com

9 8 7 6 5 4 3 2 1

Cover photo by Gary Crandall (www.dancingcrane.com/): Dear Hearts. Rehabilitator
Cec Sanders (Wet Mountain Wildlife Rehabilitation in Florence, Colorado) feeds orphaned
fawns using the multiple fawn feeder (MFF), which was designed by her husband, Tom.

Library of Congress Cataloging-in-Publication Data
Jacobs, Shannon K.
    Healers of the wild: rehabilitating injured and orphaned wildlife /
Shannon K. Jacobs.—2nd ed.
        p. cm.
Includes bibliographical references (p.   ).
    ISBN 1-55566-284-6
  1. Wildlife rehabilitators. 2. Wildlife rehabilitation. 3. Wildlife
rehabilitators—United States. 4. Wildlife rehabilitation—United
States I. Title.
    SF996.45.J33 2003
    639.9'6—dc21   2003000595

Printed in the United States by
Johnson Printing
1880 South 57th Court
Boulder, Colorado 80301

Printed on ECF paper with soy ink

Contents

This book is dedicated to wildlife rehabilitators,
whose compassion for innocent creatures
graces all human hearts.

A Note from the Publisher

We first learned of Shannon Jacobs and her book, *Healers of the Wild*, from a review in the local newspaper. Intrigued, we approached Shannon and asked to distribute her self-published book. She accepted, and we've been honored to list her book in our catalog. When it came time to revise the book and bring it up to date, we offered to assume the role of publisher, which would allow us to participate with her in every aspect of the creation of this new edition. She was delighted.

Together we worked to refine the organization of the book and add new material. The project became intensely personal for Shannon with the sudden illness and death of her husband, George, shortly before this edition went to press. *Healers of the Wild* reflects the love and passion George and Shannon have always felt for wildlife. The book would never have been created without George's ongoing support, enthusiasm, and pride. We are proud to be a part of this project.

We would like to thank The Fund for Animals, especially Laura Simon, Urban Wildlife Director. The Fund has permitted us to include many of its effective, humane, innovative, and long-term solutions for solving wildlife problems. The suggestions are especially relevant today, and even more so for the future, due to the continuing loss of wildlife habitat.

Healers of the Wild is appropriate for readers from age ten and up. This second edition offers many more resources, especially online.

Foreword

This book is a godsend for everyone who loves and respects wildlife and hates to see animals suffer. People who read this book will learn how to help orphaned or injured wild animals so that they will be able to react correctly and legally to a situation until a wildlife rehabilitator can be contacted.

For more than twenty years, wildlife rehabilitators have answered hundreds of thousands of phone calls from people who want to know what to do when they find wildlife in trouble. People's compassion for each animal is heartwarming. Sometimes it is what keeps us going through trying times.

Healers of the Wild describes many wildlife rehabilitators of today—who we are, what we do, and a little about why we do what we do. No longer is it enough to mean well and have good intentions. We now share the knowledge to provide *proper* medical care, housing, nutrition, captive management, and release conditioning while striving to respect and preserve the wildness of those entrusted to our care.

There is no other book quite like this one. Shannon's easy-to-read style weaves together stories, photographs, facts, and advice. The stories and photographs are about real wild animals that have been helped by many dedicated volunteers and caring people working together across the United States. Some of these stories have had happy endings, and some have not.

When we realize some of the problems that wild animals face, we can help *prevent* injuries, poisonings, and orphaned youngsters. The more we understand wild creatures, the more we respect them and want to help them. The more we learn, the better we can help them. Those who understand wildlife will be able to tell when a rescue is necessary. Just as importantly, they will know when a rescue is *not* necessary.

Charts at the end of the book guide us through the thought process of determining what to do when finding an injured or orphaned baby bird or mammal. Other valuable resources include lists of wildlife rehabilitation organizations, state and federal agencies, and suggested books and videos.

We all want to do what is best for the wild animals we encounter. Each injured or orphaned wild creature found by a person who reads this book will have a better chance of surviving and being returned to the wild where it belongs.

Thank you, Shannon.

Elaine Thrune
President, National Wildlife
Rehabilitators Association, 1987–2002

1
Who Helps Wildlife?

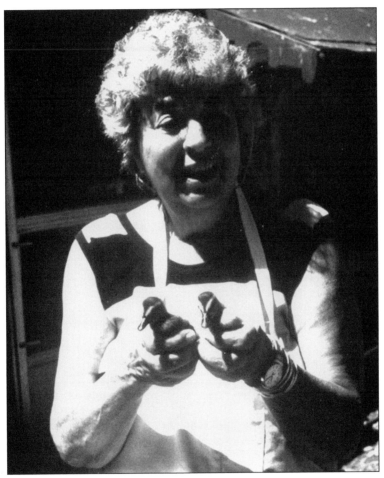

Heart of Gold. *These orphaned ducklings are among the hundreds of birds Anna Gold (Thornton, Colorado) rehabilitates every spring and summer. (Shannon K. Jacobs)*

What's Your Wildlife IQ?

What would you do if you …

- Mowed over a nest of baby bunnies in your yard?
- Discovered a raccoon family living in your attic?
- Found a fawn curled up alone in a meadow?
- Spotted a baby bird hopping in your flower bed?

These are familiar meetings between people and wild animals, and many people aren't sure what to do.

Raccoon Rascals. What would you do if you found these cute youngsters in the woods? (Shannon K. Jacobs)

"I would take the animal home."

First, know that it's *against the law* to take wild animals home. Also, picking up wild animals often can harm them more than help them.

"I would take the animal to my vet."

Many veterinarians can't or won't treat wild animals, and in some states they must have special licenses to do so.

"I would give the animal to a zoo."

Zoos rarely take wildlife. Usually they don't have room, and zoo officials worry about diseases that wildlife carry.

Fortunately, there are wildlife rehabilitators, or "rehabbers," all over the country who help.

Wildlife Rehabilitators

Wildlife rehabilitators rescue and rehabilitate sick, injured, and orphaned wildlife and release healthy animals back to the wild. Surprisingly, most rehabilitators are not veterinarians—they are musicians, teachers, nurses, homemakers, retired people, biologists, and bakers, among many others. Because they've had special training, rehabilitators know the best ways to care for wildlife. Sometimes that means leaving an animal alone instead of rescuing it.

Rehabilitators also know what wild animals need in the way of food, housing, or medical treatment. They've developed the skills necessary to safely handle wild creatures, and they've learned how to keep wild animals wild.

Rehabilitators are necessary because wild animals are in trouble. More and more people are moving into wildlife habitats, and when land is cleared for houses, businesses, or farming, wildlife homes and foods are destroyed. Wild animals then become displaced, injured, orphaned, or killed.

Rehabilitators estimate that at least 90 percent of the wild animals they treat are injured because of human activities. The most common causes of such injuries are collisions with human-made objects such as cars, boats, airplanes, windows, and towers; cat and dog attacks; shooting and trapping; poisoning; litter; and pollution.

Displaced. *Sandy Cate, director of Adobe Mountain Wildlife Center in Phoenix, Arizona, holds a ring-tailed cat that was accidentally dug out of its burrow by workers laying phone lines. (Shannon K. Jacobs)*

State Wildlife Agencies

Many people think that state wildlife officials or veterinarians are responsible for helping injured and orphaned creatures, but that's not true. State wildlife agencies manage populations of wildlife, but they are not prepared or equipped to take care of individual animals.

Veterinarians

Until recently, veterinarians were not trained to treat wild animals. Now most veterinary schools offer some classes in wildlife medicine, but decent-paying jobs in the field are rare.

Dr. John Huckabee is one of just a few veterinarians who work full-time in wildlife rehabilitation. He is wildlife veterinarian for the Wildlife Department of the Progressive Animal Welfare Society (PAWS) in Lynnwood, Washington.

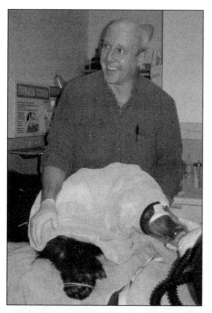

"I went to veterinary school because I wanted to work with wildlife," Huckabee said. "After graduation I moved to Houston. I was amazed to find that there was no place for injured wildlife in the fourth largest city in the nation."

Huckabee tried unsuccessfully for several years to start such a place. His hard work paid off a few years later, though, when he was hired by Harris County to develop the Wildlife Center of Harris County Precinct 4, where he was director and staff veterinarian.

A Busy Schedule. Dr. John R. Huckabee with an anesthetized bear on the surgery table prior to its pre-release examination on the day of its release. This was a bear that was raised and rehabilitated at the PAWS Wildlife Center in Lynnwood, Washington. (Sheridan Thomas)

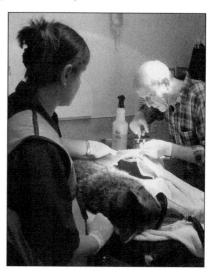

Dr. Huckabee (center) with the same bear at the winter den release site later that day, with PAWS Wildlife Department Naturalist Kevin Mack (right)and a wildlife biologist with the Washington Department of Fish and Wildlife (left), after placing a state (WDFW) eartag in the bear's ear. The sedated bear was placed in the winter den immediately following capture of this image. (Sheridan Thomas)

Dr. Huckabee suturing the damaged foot of a coyote, with PAWS Wildlife Rehabilitation Manager Jennifer Convy monitoring anesthesia. (PAWS)

Today the county supports the center by paying the salaries for a veterinarian and a veterinary technician. The county also funds the space in 320-acre Burroughs Park, office support, supplies and equipment, and utilities. Other money must be raised through donations, grants, and volunteers.

Huckabee would like to see more county-supported rehabilitation centers. "The Wildlife Center of Harris County is a good model for other counties that would like to do this," he said.

Feathered, Furred, and Scaled

Some wildlife rehabilitators work with birds, mammals, and reptiles. A few specialize in certain creatures, such as bats, raptors, or marine animals. Because so many wild creatures live around cities, a lot of rehabilitators take care of urban wildlife such as raccoons, foxes, skunks, opossums, and squirrels. A small number of brave souls care for animals most of us would avoid—porcupines, bobcats, mountain lions, bears, and badgers.

Like many rehabilitators, Phylis Rollins grew up loving animals. But what nudged her into rehabilitation was her cat.

Early one morning the cat caught a bird and turned it loose in Rollins's bedroom. Rollins spent hours trying to find help for the injured bird. Finally she found a place that took wildlife, and she rushed the bird

Prickly Porcupine. A few brave souls take care of wildlife most people would avoid. (Greenwood Wildlife Sanctuary)

there. A volunteer admitted it to the center. Although very impressed with the place, Rollins didn't give it much more thought.

The next Sunday, her cat brought her another feathered trophy. Rollins promptly returned to the center and handed over the second bird. This time she also filled out an application to volunteer. It was her first step toward becoming a rehabilitator (and the last time her cat brought home a bird).

Rollins worked at the wildlife center once a week, feeding baby animals and cleaning cages. Just when she began to wish for more challenging work, the center admitted a mother opossum that had been badly tangled in a barbed-wire fence. The opossum didn't live, but four of her babies did. After the babies were cleaned up, the director asked Rollins to take care of them.

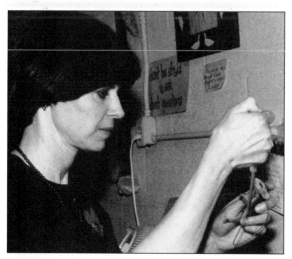

Baby Food. As a volunteer rehabilitator, Phylis Rollins learned to tube-feed baby opossums. (Phylis Rollins)

That project sparked Rollins's passion for opossums. She learned everything possible about the marvelous marsupials. Soon she became the opossum team leader, responsible for training other volunteers as well as rescuing, rehabilitating, and releasing opossums.

Because of her other work rescuing turtles and tortoises, Rollins has been interviewed for television, radio, and newspapers—a big accomplishment for a very shy person.

Becoming a Rehabilitator

How do people become healers of the wild? Many begin as volunteers, like Rollins, working with experienced rehabilitators and veterinarians.

Jaws. Rollins took care of a car-hit opossum named Jaws, whose mouth was wired shut temporarily to allow the fractured jaws to heal. (Phylis Rollins)

State Permits

In most states, people must become licensed or obtain permits before they can rehabilitate wild animals on their own. This system ensures that people have the proper knowledge, skills, and facilities to care for wildlife. Volunteers, however, don't need permits as long as they work at centers that are licensed.

States may require that rehabilitators pass courses in wildlife rehabilitation or prove their knowledge of wildlife, state laws, and handling of wild animals. Sometimes state wildlife inspectors visit homes to make sure rehabilitators have the correct cages, enclosures, and equipment as well as veterinary help. Beginners may have to work for a certain period of time with experienced rehabilitators.

Federal Permits

In order to rehabilitate migratory birds, rehabilitators must have special permits, which are granted by the U.S. Fish and Wildlife Service (USFWS). People who rehabilitate endangered species also need special permits from USFWS.

The National Marine Fisheries Service (NMFS) oversees the rescue and rehabilitation of marine mammals. NMFS issues permits, which are called Letters of Authorization (LOA), to qualified centers. The centers must prove that they have experienced staff and veterinary help, proper equipment, an appropriate place to keep the animals, and money to pay for expenses.

Frequently Asked Questions

Q: *How many rehabilitators are there?*
A: At least six thousand wildlife rehabilitators are licensed or granted

Silver Plume. People who rehabilitate endangered species or migratory birds need special permits from the U.S. Fish and Wildlife Service. (Heidi Bucknam)

Dolphin Helper. Lynne Stringer works with Noodge, a rough-toothed dolphin. Stringer is lead animal technician with Wildlife Rescue of the Florida Keys, a center with a permit from National Marine Fisheries Service to rescue and rehabilitate marine mammals. (Becky Barron)

permits by state wildlife agencies. A few thousand have federal permits to rehabilitate migratory birds and endangered species.

Q: How many wild animals do rehabilitators help?

A: Rehabilitators directly care for hundreds of thousands of wild creatures every year. Indirectly, they assist millions more by educating people about wildlife issues and helping them deal humanely with human-wildlife conflicts. They also work very hard to preserve wildlife habitats.

Q: Who pays rehabilitators?

A: Most are not paid for their work at all. In fact, they often pay out of their own pockets for food, cages, and medicines. Many rehabilitators form nonprofit organizations so they can ask for donations from individuals and businesses. Such donations are tax-deductible.

Q: How much does it cost to rehabilitate wildlife?

A. It is expensive. One raptor rehabilitator estimated that she spends $350 to return one bird of prey to the wild. Another healer who cares for birds, mammals, and reptiles pays about $8,000 a year for wildlife expenses. Costs for rehabilitating one orphaned harbor seal pup can run up to $1,500.

Expenses include food, housing, medical supplies, and veterinary care. Also included are rents or leases, insurance, phones, vehicles, gas, electricity, and heating.

Nonprofits. *Many rehabilitators form nonprofit wildlife organizations, such as this one in Key West. (Shannon K. Jacobs)*

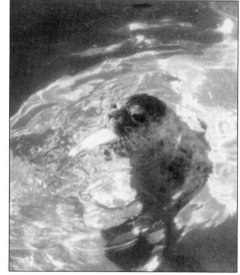

Harbor Seal Pup. *It can cost as much as $1,500 to raise and release one orphaned baby seal. (Caroline Brawner)*

Rehabilitation centers sometimes receive donated items from companies, such as dog food from pet stores, fruits and vegetables from grocery stores, or building supplies from lumber companies. Such donations can save them thousands of dollars a year.

Some average costs and hospital days at Greenwood Wildlife Rehabilitation Sanctuary in Longmont, Colorado:

Baby bird: . . . . $1 a day for 30 days
Baby rabbit, squirrel, or prairie dog: $2 a day for 40 days
Baby fox, coyote, or raccoon: . . . . . . $3 a day for 120 days

Q: *How do rehabilitators learn how to care for wild animals?*

A: Typically, they get a lot of hands-on experience and share information among themselves. They also take classes, attend conferences and workshops, and constantly read books and articles about wildlife biology and treatment.

Two national organizations—National Wildlife Rehabilitators Association (NWRA) and International Wildlife Rehabilitation Council (IWRC)—provide classes for beginners and experienced rehabilitators. State wildlife rehabilitation associations also offer continuing education courses.

Q: *How much time does it take to rehabilitate wildlife?*

A: It is a serious commitment that takes a great deal of time, especially during the wild and crazy times of the year, such as spring and summer. Anyone interested in becoming a rehabilitator should first talk it over with (and volunteer with) experienced people.

Feed Me! Feed Me! *It takes a lot of time and energy to rehabilitate wildlife. The animals need frequent feedings, warmth, attention, companionship with their own species, proper enclosures, and thorough survival training. (Greenwood Wildlife Rehabilitation Sanctuary)*

2
Rescue—The First Step

Wet and Wild. *Volunteers from The Marine Mammal Center (left to right) Vi Brown, Guthrum Purdin, and Rebecca Duerr rescue California sea lions entangled in fishing nets. They take the sea lions to safer ground, remove the nets, and release healthy animals. If badly injured, the sea lions may be admitted for treatment. (© 1997 The Marine Mammal Center/Photo: Ken Bach)*

Anyone Can Help

"Hey, look, an owl!" a man in downtown Denver cried. He pointed to a cross-walk signal. Upon it sat a beautiful great horned owl.

All morning, people on their way to work stopped to stare at the bird. Television reporters arrived in the afternoon to film the urban owl for the evening news. Finally someone got worried about the bird and called the Colorado Division of Wildlife. The division contacted Birds of Prey Foundation (BOP). Michael Judish, a volunteer trained in raptor rescue, quickly showed up to help. He explained to the crowd that the bird wasn't behaving normally.

Footing Protection. *It's important to wear gloves when handling birds of prey. Even young ones, such as this great horned owl, can slash with their talons. (Critter Alley)*

"Owls should avoid people," he said. "Something's wrong when a wild animal lets you get this close."

To prove his point, Judish stepped up next to the raptor. The bird didn't move away or turn around. That made its capture easy. Judish wore gloves to pick up the bird so the owl wouldn't foot (slash) him with its talons.

When BOP director Sigrid Ueblacker examined the owl (named StopGo), she discovered why he had put up with crowds of people and screeching traffic—he was blind. StopGo had probably collided with a car while hunting a mouse. StopGo's head injury was temporary, though. The owl recovered completely and was released a few weeks later.

Experience Not Needed

You don't have to be an experienced rescuer to assist wildlife; anyone can help. For kids, the most important thing to do is *get an adult right away.* Adults should immediately call a wildlife rehabilitator.

If someone had contacted Birds of Prey Foundation as soon as StopGo was spotted downtown, the owl would have been rescued much sooner. Rehabilitators recognize abnormal behavior in animals and know when it's important to capture an animal quickly, not only for its own safety but for the protection of the humans who encounter it. Rehabbers give the best advice on when to rescue and when *not* to. The latter expertise helps to prevent the many unnecessary rescues that happen with young animals.

Baby-Nappers

Did you know that very few baby animals that appear to have been abandoned are true orphans? Unfortunately, kindhearted people often pick up baby animals, thinking they need help. But without a background in the natural history of wildlife, most of us are not able to make good judgments about such matters. If you saw a baby bird hopping on the ground, for example, you might think it was an orphan. But more than likely it would be a fledgling (young bird learning to fly). Sometimes you can identify fledglings by their short tail feathers, fuzzy down on their heads, and clumsy movements. While practicing flying skills, fledglings spend several days hopping around on the ground. Normally their parents are nearby, feeding and caring for the young birds until they can find their own food. Fledglings need help only if they are sick or injured or if cats, dogs, or people are a threat to them.

Because they look so helpless, fawns and baby seals are frequently "rescued." People don't understand that it's normal behavior for these creatures to lie quietly in grass or on a beach and wait for their mothers. Usually the mothers are feeding nearby. Fawns' spotted coats help them blend in with bushes and grass so predators can't see them. Fawns usually do not have a scent, so predators cannot smell them. If you pick up a healthy baby, you are taking it away from its best chance for survival—its mother. Fawns and seal pups need help only if they are crying, injured, or in danger from predators, or if you know for sure that the mother is dead.

Family reunions do happen, even when baby animals are rescued by mistake. But they take a lot of time

Fuzzy-Headed Fledglings. *These oriole youngsters are learning how to fly. Their parents still feed them. (Karen Von den Deale)*

Don't Rescue Me. *Most baby seal rescues are unnecessary because the mothers have not abandoned their young. They are feeding close by. (Caroline Brawner)*

Mom Knows. *A fawn's lack of scent protects it from predators. (Critter Alley)*

and energy. For instance, when a woman rescued ten ducklings crossing a busy street in Boulder, Colorado, she also tried to capture the mother duck. She couldn't catch the mother, so she took the babies to Greenwood Wildlife Rehabilitation Sanctuary. Fortunately, she remembered exactly where she had picked up the babies. Elaine Myers, an animal care coordinator at Greenwood, immediately took the ducklings back to where they had been rescued and searched for the mother. Greenwood already had twenty-two ducklings in the intensive care unit, and ten more would have severely overloaded the sanctuary's capabilities.

Sitting Ducks. *Keeping Mom and her young together is very important. (Shannon K. Jacobs)*

When Myers saw two mallard ducks paddling down the nearby creek, she held up the box of peeping babies, hoping the pair was the parents. They weren't. Two more mallards floated by, and Myers again showed off the fuzzy ducklings.

The female duck quacked and slowly approached. Myers set down five ducklings, and the female duck herded them into the creek. She then released the rest of the ducklings, and they swam wildly to catch up with their mother and siblings, peeping in their high-pitched voices. Finally the re-united family floated off, the father mallard staying in the rear to make sure no babies strayed.

In another case in Scottsdale, Arizona, five owl babies (from three different families) were brought to Liberty Wildlife Rehabilitation Foundation—all in one week. The owlets were healthy, so Liberty volunteer Peggy Kavookjian made it her mission to return them to their nests. She located the nests by re-turning to the places where the babies had been found and looking for owl pellets under trees. Owls spit up the pellets, which are made of fur, teeth, and bones that haven't been digested. The sausage-shaped pellets can be found under almost any tree where a family of owls has roosted.

Following pellet clues, Kavookjian found a palm tree with an adult owl in it. She left the baby owl in nearby bushes. When she checked back the next day, she saw the fledgling sitting next to its parent.

Three other nestling owls had fallen from their damaged nest, which was located inside the arm of a saguaro cactus. Using a ladder to climb the tall, bristly cactus, Kavookjian and her husband re-paired the nest. Then they returned the baby owls to their rebuilt home under the watchful eyes of the mother owl.

The final owlet had been found on private property. Kavookjian and the owner walked the land, searching for owl clues. When they spot-ted pellets under a tree, they also saw the nest. Kavookjian left the fledgling at the bottom of the owl tree, where the parents would find it.

This project was a lot of work for Kavookjian, but it was well worth it because young owls are best raised by their parents.

Mystery Clues? Owl pellets.
(Shannon K. Jacobs)

Loving Wildlife to Death

Some people rescue wild creatures by taking them home. They think they can care for the animals properly because they love them. But love is not enough. Caring for wild animals is very different from raising cats and dogs. Ignorance about their needs causes permanent injuries, suffering, and death.

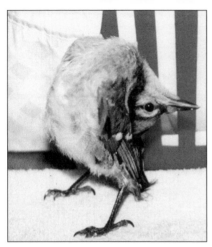

Imagine if you were hurt in a car accident. Would you want someone off the street, with no medical background, taking you home? Or would you want help from a medical expert in a hospital? It's no different with wildlife. They deserve the best professional care possible.

It is against the law in most states to keep wild animals without permits, even if you plan to release them. These laws were created to protect animals from people who steal them, sell them, or harm them by taking them home. They also were meant to help protect public health because wild animals carry diseases and parasites (fleas, ticks, lice, or worms).

Deformed Bluejay. This young bird was raised illegally in someone's home and fed the wrong diet, which caused its bone deformity. The bird had to be euthanized. (Karen Von den Deale)

Finding Wildlife Rehabilitators

It is a good idea for everyone—families, schools, businesses, and community organizations—to keep a list of nearby wildlife rehabilitators. Call or write your state wildlife agency and ask for the names of rehabilitators who care for birds and mammals. Sometimes one person will handle both. State wildlife agencies are listed alphabetically in the last section of this book.

If there are no rehabilitators in your town or city, ask your state wildlife agency to give you the name of the nearest rehabilitator. Even if that person is a few hundred miles away, he or she can give you advice over the phone if you call for help.

If you're traveling in another city or state, call the state wildlife agency listed in the phone book. You can also check the yellow pages for "Wildlife Rescue" or "Animal Shelter." If re-

Where's Mom? These orphaned raccoons will get the best care possible at a rehabilitation center. (Critter Alley)

habilitators are not listed in a phone book, contact any of these places and ask for the nearest wildlife rehabilitator:

- Humane Society
- Audubon Society
- Wild Bird Centers or Wild Birds Unlimited
- City animal-control officers
- Veterinarians (wildlife/exotic)
- Highway Patrol
- Coast Guard or Marine Patrol
- U.S. Fish and Wildlife Service (for migratory birds or endangered species)
- Fund for Animals Urban Wildlife Hotline: 203-389-4411

If you find an animal that looks injured or orphaned, observe the animal carefully, then call a rehabilitator before taking any other action. If the rehabilitator decides that the animal needs help, she or he will arrange for its rescue, either picking up the animal or asking a volunteer (maybe the caller) to take it to a rehabilitation center.

Anyone who decides to help with a rescue should always consider personal safety first. Frightened wild animals bite, scratch, kick, or stab. A rehabilitator can explain how to capture and handle the animal safely. Different special capture methods are used for different species and ages of animals as well as for specific situations. No one should try to rescue adult animals without guidance from a rehabilitator because they are too dangerous to handle without professional help.

If you choose not to rescue an animal, there are other ways to help until rescuers arrive. Sick or injured animals will try to hide in bushes, drains, or tall

Ice-Pick Sharp. *Rehabilitator Jean Lisle carefully holds an injured western grebe, a water bird known for its strong neck and lightning-fast stabs. (Untrained people should not rescue water birds without a rehabilitator's help. The birds can inflict serious wounds, such as putting out an eye.) (Catherine Hurlbutt)*

grass if they are able to move. A person who watches the animal can tell rescuers exactly where it is hiding. Another way to help is to put a plastic laundry basket or cardboard box (with air holes) over the creature to keep it in one place and protect it from predators until help arrives.

For detailed steps on how to rescue baby birds and mammals, turn to Appendix A.

Ready to Roll. A quick-thinking rescuer placed this mourning dove inside a soft-drink container before calling a rehabilitator. This prevented the bird from flapping around and making its broken wing worse. (Catherine Hurlbutt)

Baby Bird Quiz

Question: Should this baby great horned owl be rescued? It is a fledgling that has left the nest, and the parents are still feeding it.

(Michael Judish)

Answer: The bird does *not* need to be rescued. As long as it is safe from predators (including cats, dogs, and people) and the parents are feeding it, the young owl is okay.

Frequently Asked Questions

Q: We brought home baby birds that fell out of their nest. What should we feed them?

A: Before you do anything (even feed them), call a rehabilitator or your state wildlife agency right away. Do not wait a few hours or days—young birds die quickly without the right care. The rehabilitator will tell you what to do with the birds. If she asks you to put the baby birds back in their nest, she will explain how to do it. If the birds are injured or cannot be returned to the nest, the rehabilitator may ask you to bring the birds to her.

Get Help. *Baby birds need professional help. If you find baby birds, call a rehabilitator. (Karen Von den Deale)*

Q: I took a nest of squirrels to a rehabilitator. A friend said I should not have carried the squirrels in my jacket. Why not?

A: Most wild animals have parasites, and some have diseases that can be passed to people and pets.

Q: Do mother animals really reject their babies if people touch them?

A: We have all heard that statement, but it is not true. Most birds have a poor sense of smell, so they do not know when their babies have been touched by people. Hence, it is okay to put baby birds back in their nests if they fall out (and if they are not injured).

Mammals do have a good sense of smell, but mammal moms will not reject their babies if people handle them as little as possible. For example, if you mowed over a nest of baby bunnies, you

Don't Handle Wildlife. *Most wild animals have fleas, lice, or ticks and also carry diseases. Leave it to the professionals. (Critter Alley)*

could repair the nest and replace the babies (if they weren't injured). The mother rabbit would keep caring for her babies as long as people stayed away from the nest.

Many wild babies do not have scents when they are born. This trait protects them from predators. Too much touching, though, can leave a human scent, which might lead predators to the nest or den.

Q: *I picked up an injured bat and took it home. When the bat bit me, the Department of Health took it away to be tested for rabies. Then they killed the bat! It didn't have rabies, so why did they kill it?*

A: Any animal that bites a person has to be checked for rabies, a deadly viral disease that all warm-blooded animals—including humans—can get from an infected animal. That is especially true if the animal is a coyote, bat, raccoon, skunk, or fox because these are rabies vector species (animals that most often get rabies and infect other animals). Checking for rabies requires killing animals that might have the disease because samples of their brains have to be tested for the virus.

Rabies Vector Species. *Coyotes, skunks, foxes, raccoons, and bats get rabies and infect others more often than other animals. (Tom Sanders)*

Rabies cannot be treated in animals, but it can be treated successfully in humans if it is caught in time. Anyone who has been exposed to rabies *should get to a doctor immediately.* (If you wait until symptoms appear, it will be too late.) Rabies is fatal without prompt treatment.

Never touch a wild bat, especially a bat on the ground. It is probably sick. Although only a tiny number of sick bats actually have rabies, it is impossible to tell what is actually wrong with a grounded bat. If you pick it up, the bat may defend itself with its teeth; then it will have to be killed and checked for rabies. So if you want to save a bat, *don't handle it.* Call your state wildlife agency immediately. If you know of a local rehabilitator who takes care of bats, call that person. People who rehabilitate bats are vaccinated against rabies and know how to protect themselves against possibly rabid animals.

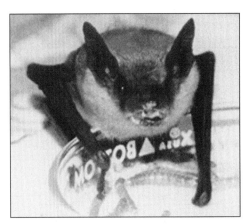

Hands Off! *Never touch a wild bat. Only a tiny number of bats actually have rabies, but there is no way of knowing what's wrong with a sick or grounded bat. (Urban Wildlife Rescue)*

Q: What should we do about box turtles crossing roads? A lot get run over.

A: If you can do it safely, carry the turtle to the other side of the road—just make sure you take it in the direction it was headed. Otherwise, it will turn around and cross the road again. Wash your hands thoroughly after handling the turtle because, like other wild animals, it may carry diseases or parasites.

Repairing Shell Damage. Often a shell can be wired or glued back together after a turtle is run over by a car. But this is not a simple procedure. Only rehabilitators or veterinarians should do it. Infections and other injuries need to be treated as well. (Critter Alley)

Q: I have heard people say we should not worry about saving common animals like pigeons and opossums. Is it a waste of energy and resources to care for animals that are not rare or endangered?

A: "Nothing deserves to suffer," said Catherine (Birdie) Hurlbutt, a bird rescuer and former rehabilitator who is a local legend in Denver, Colorado. "Every living creature deserves humane treatment."

Hurlbutt has devoted her life to helping wild creatures, especially birds. "What would a child learn about compassion if she brought me a sick bird and I refused to help it, just because it was common?" she asked. Her mission is to show children that adults really care about wild creatures. During summers, she has driven as many as a hundred miles a day, rescuing feathered friends. That's a lot of driving for a ninety-year-old woman with an oxygen tank, and it explains why her car has traveled more than 300,000 miles!

Birdie. Catherine Hurlbutt is a best friend to birds. (Shannon K. Jacobs)

Q: *Rehabilitation sounds like a lot of fun. Is it?*

A: Taking care of wild creatures is definitely fun, but only about half the time. The other half is difficult because about 50 percent of the animals either die or are beyond help when they are admitted. The work can be emotionally draining, physically tiring, and discouraging. Some rehabilitators burn out because they have overdone it physically and emotionally. When that happens, they may have to cut back on the number of their animal patients or leave rehabilitation work altogether for a while.

Part of what new rehabbers need to learn is how to take care of themselves *and* find time and energy to cope with difficult decisions, demanding schedules, and lack of money.

Look at Me, Ma! *Wild critters, especially young ones, provide lots of laughs for rehabilitators. The animals' crazy antics help make up for hard work, emotional rough times, and no pay. (Urban Wildlife Rescue)*

3
Rehabilitation—The Second Step

Cat Attack. *This infant gray squirrel suffered a broken leg when attacked by a cat. Fortunately, the little creature was rehabilitated successfully and later released. (Karen Von den Deale)*

Hospitals for Wildlife

Many rehabilitation centers are home-based, meaning they are located in rehabilitators' homes and backyards. Others are like clinics, housed in separate buildings. A few are part of nature centers or universities.

Generous Vets. *Dr. Lee Eggleston operates on an eagle with a broken leg. (Sigrid Ueblacker)*

Coons Keeping Cool. *Housing animals of the same species, such as these orphaned raccoons, together helps them stay wild and learn from each other. (Shannon Brink)*

An animal brought to a center is examined by a rehabilitator and given first aid, if needed. Very young or chilled babies may go into incubators for warmth. Newly admitted animals are quarantined to protect other animals from diseases the new patients might be carrying.

Rehabilitators keep a chart for each patient, just as in human hospitals. Since volunteers often work in shifts, a person on each shift writes notes about the animals' conditions, feedings, treatments, and medications. This procedure keeps everyone up-to-date.

Rehabilitators take animals with diseases, broken bones, or internal injuries to veterinarians. An animal that undergoes surgery is returned to the rehab center for recovery.

Some large centers have their own wildlife veterinarians, but most rehabilitators work with local veterinarians, many of whom donate their services.

Crafting Cages

When animals become well or old enough to take care of themselves, they are moved from indoor cages to outdoor enclosures. Several animals of the same species live together, getting used to each other and spending less time with humans.

Animals kept in the wrong kind of cages can develop serious or fatal injuries. Some sad examples are wild birds that rehabilitators receive after they have been confiscated by law enforcement officials from people who captured them illegally. These bird-nappers often keep the birds in wire cages, and wild birds do not sit quietly in confinement. They break bones and damage feathers as they frantically try to escape.

Rehabilitators often keep newly hatched baby birds in berry boxes, margarine containers, or aquariums that are placed inside incubators for warmth. Older baby birds are put in cardboard or wooden boxes covered with soft netting or in small, nonwire cages.

Each stage of an animal's recovery requires different space. For instance, an owl with a broken wing might do better at first in a small, dark cage, where it can calm down and rest. Later, with the wing healed, the owl might be moved to a flight cage (a specialized large outdoor enclosure) where it could develop the muscle strength and coordination necessary for flying.

On the Mend. *A roomy flight cage enables a snowy owl to strengthen its flying muscles. (Sigrid Ueblacker)*

Good Old Bear

Some enclosures need to be very sturdy, especially if they hold large animals. Sally Maughan (Idaho Black Bear Rehab, Inc.) spent several thousand dollars of her own money to construct a strong main enclosure for adult bears and a pen for cubs.

Most of the bear cubs Maughan has rehabilitated were orphaned when their mothers were hit by cars, killed during spring or fall bear hunts, or poached. When the cubs are brought to Maughan, they may weigh only five pounds. By December, when they are ready to den for the winter, the bears are as big as Maughan and weigh sixty-five to one hundred pounds!

Big Guys. *Large animals, such as these bears, need very strong enclosures. (Sally Maughan)*

Orphaned Cubs. *Most of the black bears Sally Maughan rehabilitates became orphaned when their mothers have been killed by hunters or by cars. (Sally Maughan)*

Griz. *A powerful black bear, Griz, dries off after his daily swim. (Sally Maughan)*

During one busy year, Maughan cared for fifteen bears. The animals stayed in a chain-link enclosure that was strong enough to support climbing cubs. Maughan entered the enclosure twice a day to feed the bears and to clean up after them. The bears were fairly predictable, with one exception—Griz, the most powerful bear she had ever rehabilitated. One day Griz grabbed Maughan in a bear hug, holding her so tightly that she could not move or turn. When Griz's sister distracted him, Maughan escaped. Although she was frightened, Maughan knew that Griz was not trying to hurt her. "He just thought I was one of the bears," she explained.

Bear Den. *Shenandoah, an eight-month-old black bear, rests in her hollow-log den. (Sally Maughan)*

Each November Maughan begins cutting back on the bears' food. She usually stops feeding them around Thanksgiving so the sleepy bears will climb inside their dens for the winter, just as wild bears do. The "dens" Maughan provides are dog houses, dog kennels, large hollow logs, and a turned-over 160-gallon swim tub. Later in the winter, with the help of wildlife officials, she moves the sleeping bears to real dens in wilderness areas. The bears sleep there until spring, when they wake up wild and free.

Marine Animals

Enclosures for marine animals such as otters, dolphins, whales, sea turtles, and seals require clean pools of water that are chemically balanced and kept at correct temperatures. Some need haul-out areas where the animals can climb out of the water, just as in the wild. Because of these complicated housing needs, only specialized rehabilitation centers or aquariums are equipped to handle captive marine animals.

Crank Up the Heat

Keeping baby animals warm is critical for their survival. Rehabbers place heating pads, lightbulbs, or hot-water bottles in parts of cages so animals can seek warmth when they need it and move away from it when they do not.

Young animals die quickly from cold. One man learned this sad lesson when he rescued two baby sandpipers whose mother had been run over by a car. He placed the baby birds in a big box and took them to a wildlife center. The man had put a wet beach towel in the box with the birds, possibly trying to cover or cushion them, but the towel chilled the babies. They arrived at the center shaking with cold. Both birds died.

For steps on what to do for orphaned animals, turn to Chapter 10.

Stressed Out

Would you be frightened if huge creatures kidnapped you and locked you in a cage, then surrounded you, baring their sharp teeth and staring at you? Naturally, captive wild creatures are terrified of us. Every

Romping on the Ramp. Steller sea lions, like all marine animals, need large enclosures in specialized centers. (© 1997 The Marine Mammal Center/ Photo: Jane Oka)

Choosing Heat. A newly hatched baby pheasant sits on top of a hot-water bottle, while a fully feathered house sparrow and kingbird (lower right) choose to stay away. (Catherine Hurlbutt)

Hideaway. Rehabilitators make sure wild animals, such as these shy foxes, have places to hide from people. These lucky critters have a snug den within their enclosure. (*Greenwood Wildlife Rehabilitation Sanctuary*)

Munched Mouse. Regular fresh meat gives wild carnivores, such as this great horned owl, important nutrients in their diet. (Frozen food is only a substitute.) (*Heidi Bucknam*)

time a human approaches, they fear for their lives.

Many wild animals die from the stress of captivity. Stress also slows down their healing processes. That's why a veterinary hospital or animal shelter full of barking dogs is a terrible place to keep wildlife. Rehabilitators try to keep animals in quiet places away from the human sights, sounds, and smells that panic them. They hang towels in front of cages to give the animals privacy, and they ask volunteers not to stare into the cages and to be quiet while working nearby.

Staring is threatening to wild animals because it is what predators do to their prey. Think of how a cougar stalks a deer, staring at it from the high grass. Think of how an eagle glares at a rabbit it plans to grab in its talons. When a human stares at a small animal, that creature thinks it is going to be eaten. Hence, out of respect and understanding, rehabilitators avoid looking directly at animals when working inside or near their cages.

Carnivore Cuisine

Rehabilitators sometimes joke that their families won't go near their wildlife freezers. If you took a peek inside, you would appreciate why wild food is stored separately from people food. Wildlife freezers are jammed with meat-eaters' delights. One wildly popular food is "mouse-cicles" (frozen mice), a supplemental food for raptors, bobcats, coyotes, foxes, and vultures, among others. Delicious when thawed and served whole, mouse-cicles can be skinned and chopped, blended, or whipped into a fabulous mouse mousse.

Roadkill Café

Other frozen treats are slabs of venison, sides of beef, or baggies stuffed with frozen rats, rabbits, quails, or chickens. Always recyclers, rehabilitators don't waste fresh meat, even roadkill. Whole animals (meat, fur, feathers, bones, and guts) are the best source of nutrients for wild carnivores.

Three cougar cubs gobbled twenty pounds of meat *every day* at Wet Mountain Wildlife Rehabilitation in southern Colorado. The rehabilitators, Cec and Tom Sanders, tossed the snarling triplets wild meat—especially venison—when it was available. Otherwise, the three-month-old cubs wolfed down car-hit cottontails and other roadkill quickly scraped up by loyal volunteers.

Costly Wild Cats. These orphaned cougar cubs gobbled twenty pounds of meat every day while being rehabilitated. Showing behavior typical of wild cats, the snarling cubs got up as high as they could—in this case onto a high platform inside their large enclosure—to get as far away from people as possible. (Tom Sanders)

Cutting Costs

It takes creativity to keep costs down. Many wild animals need meat, but the fresh and frozen stuff is expensive to buy. A mouse or small rat can cost $1 apiece. Multiply that by six to figure what a great horned owl typically eats in a day. In one rehabilitation center, raptors chow down on twenty-five thousand mice a year!

To cut expenses, some centers raise their own colonies of rats, mice, rabbits, and quail to feed the wildlife. Many grow earthworms and mealworms (beetle larvae) as well.

Joan Hughes (Volunteers for Wildlife, Westbury, New York) keeps packets of smelts (small, silvery fish) in her freezer for seagulls. "Gulls will eat anything in the wild," she said. "But in captivity, they want nothing but smelts."

D. McCoy

Hughes freezes blueberries for berry-loving birds such as cedar waxwings. For insect-eating birds, she raises mealworms, but she also buys live crickets and earthworms.

Rehabilitators' communities sometimes help out too. When a California rehabilitation center became desperate for raptor food, fifteen 4-H club members saved the day by trapping and freezing hundreds of rodents. Occasionally ranchers donate a dead (nondiseased) cow, or hunters haul in a freshly bagged antelope or elk.

One raptor rehabilitator claimed that she learned to "quarter a road-killed deer in five minutes" to take advantage of fresh carcasses dropped off by wildlife officials.

Learning About Wild Foods

Sick, orphaned, and injured creatures need good nutrition in order to heal and grow. Rehabbers spend a lot of time learning about the foods their wild patients eat in nature. They then teach the orphans about these foods. Otherwise, the young animals could starve after release.

Human food can make baby animals sick enough to die. It often causes malnutrition. Some problems of malnutrition—weak bones, poorly developed feathers, and blindness—can become permanent conditions, if the animals even survive to release.

Cow's milk is one of the worst foods anyone can feed baby animals. It makes them sick and can kill them.

Frequent Feathered Feeders

It would be much easier to feed baby birds if they took bottles, but how can birds suck without lips? Besides, their parents

Caught One! A young kingfisher catches a fish in a dish. Rehabilitators must take the place of parents, teaching orphaned birds how to catch or find food. (Karen Von den Deale)

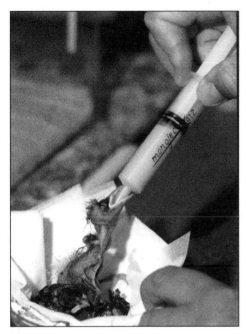

Nestlings. *Baby birds need to be fed every twenty to thirty minutes, dawn to dusk. (Critter Alley)*

Feeding Frenzy. *Volunteer Janet Teglas feeds a few of the thirty-plus orphaned grackles at Wild Care. Every spring and summer, volunteers care for hundreds of baby birds. (Karen Von den Deale)*

don't give them milk. The adults drop (or stuff) insects, seeds, fruits, or meat into the babies' begging mouths or re-gurgitate food that has been partially digested.

Rehabilitators feed each baby bird by hand at first. They use syringes or eye-droppers to give the babies formula. When the baby birds grow bigger, rehab-bers use toothpicks, forceps, or fingers to feed them the kinds of foods they will eat in the wild. These include worms, seeds, fish, berries, or chunks of meat, depending on the species.

Wild bird parents—and rehabilitators—are kept hopping from dawn until dusk, feeding nestlings as well as fledglings. Every fifteen to thirty minutes, babies have to be fed and nests cleaned. Imagine a room full of berry baskets wriggling with tiny, naked birds, their gaping beaks shrieking, cheeping, and peeping for food. As soon as a volunteer feeds one row of begging babies, it's time to start all over again. No wonder rehabilitators are thankful that most birds sleep at night!

Mammal Meals

A baby mammal needs formula that is just like its mother's milk. However, finding a substitute for mother's milk isn't easy. (Cow's milk isn't the answer, and neither is human infant formula—both cause serious problems, even death.) For many years rehabilitators whipped up their own recipes. Now a few companies make and sell different baby animal formulas.

Most young mammals need to eat every few hours, day and night. Some, like raccoons and squirrels, will take formula from a bottle, eyedropper, or syringe. But others, such as baby opossums and seriously injured animals, might have to be tube-fed if they are not able to suck. Rehabbers do this by carefully passing a narrow tube through the animal's mouth into its stomach. Formula is slowly dribbled into the stomach through the tube.

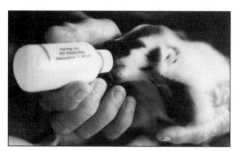

Feisty Mammals. Even baby badgers need mother's milk or the next best thing—formula. (Tom Sanders)

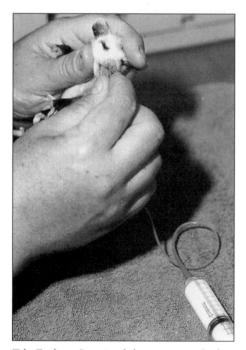

Tube Feedings. Sometimes baby opossums need to be tube-fed. (Critter Alley)

A Brave Plunge for Whales

Even sick marine mammals may need to be tube-fed—but who has the courage to tube a whale? Becky Barron does. As director of Wildlife Rescue of the Florida Keys, Barron has helped rescue and rehabilitate several whales and dolphins.

With great trust, Barron sticks her hand (and arm) down the whales' throats, passing a tube the size of a garden hose into their stomachs. Then she pours in fresh, blenderized fish.

Needles and Pills

If animals refuse to eat, fluids and medicines can be given through a needle intravenously or subcutaneously. Pills are more difficult to administer, so rehabilitators often crush medicines and hide them in tempting foods.

Tricky Treats. Deborah Halin, Lowry Park Zoo's assistant curator of Florida mammals, feeds high-protein pellets to a recovering manatee. Vitamins are hidden inside the tasty treats. (Bill Munoz)

Bushels of Wild Babies

Why is spring the wildest, craziest time of the year for wildlife rehabilitators? Because it's "baby season," a time when most wild animals give birth.

Spring is also when people pick up thousands of wild babies, assuming the little creatures have been abandoned. These well-meaning people take the babies to rehabilitators, who must then fill in for moms and dads.

The work never stops—feeding dozens of babies; cleaning them up and keeping them warm; then teaching them to hunt, find food, groom themselves, fly, swim, hide, and avoid humans.

Some babies taken from their mothers do not survive, which is why rehabilitators educate people about when to help (and *not* help) suspected orphans. A baby animal's best chance for survival—always—is its mother.

No Spring Break. Babies need to be cared for, whether they're real orphans or not. (Lynne McCoy)

Substitute Moms. Volunteers feed orphaned babies, spring and summer. Incubators in the background keep babies warm. (Critter Alley)

Imprinting

Baby animals learn very early to identify with (think they're the same species as) their mothers. This process, called imprinting, helps young animals survive. When humans raise young wild birds, there is always the risk that the birds will imprint on a person instead of their own species. Then the birds may grow up thinking that they too are human. Human-imprinted birds sometimes do not want to hang around or mate with their own species. If released, they often seek out people and become a nuisance or a danger. For this reason many birds (especially raptors) that have imprinted on humans cannot be returned to the wild.

Acoma. Because he's imprinted on people, Acoma can never be released back to the wild. (George Jackson)

One example is Acoma, a red-tailed hawk that landed on a man's shoulder while the man was cooking chicken in his backyard. The frightened man wisely contacted Liberty Wildlife Rehabilitation Foundation in Scottsdale, Arizona.

Like other too-friendly raptors, Acoma was human-imprinted: someone had stolen him from his nest and raised him. However, he wasn't fed the kind of food a hawk needs to grow strong bones and straight wings, so Acoma became weak and sick. Later, either the hawk escaped or his caretaker carelessly released him. Acoma immediately scouted out his favorite species—humans.

Because his attraction to people is unsafe, Acoma now lives permanently at Liberty Wildlife. He helps other birds by teaching people about the tragedy of stealing wildlife from the wild.

Preventing Human Imprinting

Rehabbers work hard to prevent wild animals from becoming tame or imprinting on humans. If possible, they raise babies of the same species together so they will bond with each other instead of with humans. When they have only one baby and cannot transfer it to another center with others of its

Substitute Mom. *An orphaned sea lion nuzzles his stuffed walrus mother, who comes complete with bottles. (© 1997 The Marine Mammal Center/Photo: Ken Bach)*

species, rehabilitators have to become very creative. To prevent a young animal from getting used to human voices, for example, a rehabber might not talk out loud to the animal. Instead she would play tapes of animal sounds, especially those of the baby's species. Mirrors might be put in a cage so the baby can see its own reflection.

Centers also might use surrogate mothers, such as stuffed animals or hand puppets, to help feed and raise babies. As long as a young animal cannot see its human caretaker, it will not get too used to people.

When rehabilitators at Wildlife Education and Rehabilitation Center (W.E.R.C.) in Morgan Hill, California, admitted Bobbie, an orphaned bobcat kitten, they were not sure what to do. They knew that other rehabilitators had prevented baby birds of prey from imprinting on them by using feathered gloves or hand puppets to care for the babies. But mammals are not fooled so easily. They have a good sense of smell (most birds don't). If the bobcat kitten smelled the humans who fed her, she would grow up associating human scent with food. Learning to trust humans would be Bobbie's death sentence because she would probably seek out people. Unfortunately, some people who fear or hate bobcats will shoot them on sight.

W.E.R.C. rehabilitators came up with their own creative solution. They made a fake-fur bobcat costume, complete with mask. Every day a volunteer became Bobbie's "mother" and

Bobbie. *How could rehabilitators keep an orphaned bobcat wild and teach her survival skills? (W.E.R.C.)*

dressed in the costume, brushing herself with sage and bay leaves to cover up her human smell. Bobbie, the first bobcat raised by a surrogate mother, successfully learned to hunt and to avoid people. Later she was ear-tagged and released in the state park where she had been found. Park rangers in the state park have spotted Bobbie several times. They report that she is healthy and very wild.

Using foster parents, adult animals that care for babies, is another way to prevent human imprinting. These animals often are the same species. Usually the adults are nonreleasable because of permanent injuries or because they are human-imprinted.

Workers at Shelby Steel, a steel-fabricating plant, called Anne Miller of Alabama Wildlife Rehabilitation Center in Birmingham to report that barn owls had nested in the ceiling insulation. The insulation had torn apart, and the nestling owls had died after falling from the nest.

Bobbie's "Mom." Every day a volunteer dressed in a bobcat costume, covered her smell with herbs, and taught Bobbie how to be a wild bobcat. (W.E.R.C.)

Miller had just taken in four orphaned barn owls about the same age as the ones who had died. She was worried about the expense of feeding them four-

teen rats a day, which would cost about $11 daily. Miller knew the wild barn owl parents could catch plenty of rats and mice, but would they keep hunting rodents for barn owl nestlings from the wildlife center that had been placed in a nearby substitute nest? It was worth a try.

Miller persuaded the manager of the building to let her

Barn Owl Orphans. Feeding these babies fourteen rats a day would cost $315 a month! (Helen Connor)

put up a nest box before the adult owls—who were roosting in another building—returned to find their babies gone. The manager agreed, and company workers installed the nest box fifty feet in the air, close to the original nesting site. Just before dusk, Miller put the four orphaned babies from the rehabilitation center into the nest box. Then she sat up all night, watching.

"For a while the adults flew around, upset and bewildered because they couldn't find their nestlings," Miller said. "Then they heard the babies in the nest box calling for food. The male flew away, obviously nervous, but the female could not stand it. She flew out, nabbed a mouse, and fed the babies. Then she hunted more rodents."

Nest Box. *Shelby Steel plant workers installed a new nest box for the owls. (Greg Crenshaw)*

The following evening, Miller returned, using her car as a blind so the owls could not see her. "By eleven o'clock, the parents had brought so much stuff, I knew the babies were okay," she said.

Miller had used foster parents before to raise babies at the wildlife center, but this was the first time she had combined foster parents with substitute babies, a substitute nest, and a substitute location! Thanks to the caring cooperation of the Shelby Steel plant people and Miller's willingness to lose a lot of sleep, the four fluffy owlets found a good home.

Expert Mousers. *Barn owls catch a dozen or more rodents a day to feed their young. (John Findlay III)*

Socialized Animals

Even adult animals can become socialized to people when they are cared for and handled. Then they lose their fear of humans. Fear of humans protects wild animals—without it, they cannot safely survive in the wild.

Too Friendly. Any wild animal that has lost its fear of humans is dangerous … and doomed. (Shannon K. Jacobs)

Imagine this: You are on a picnic in the mountains. Suddenly you see a black bear waddle toward you. He is completely unafraid. Someone has raised him from a cub, and he is used to people giving him food, but you don't know that. All you see is a huge, wild bear coming toward you. Are people safe around this bear? Is the bear safe around people? What do you think will happen to this friendly bear?

Frequently Asked Questions

Q: *Some people I know who shoot birds for target practice claim that birds don't feel pain. Is that true?*

A: All creatures feel pain. The difference is that wild animals don't show it. In the wild, any injury, sickness, or disability draws attention to an animal, so the wounded suffer in silence to protect their lives. But they still suffer.

Contact your state wildlife agency or a wildlife rehabilitator about this problem. The people who are doing the shooting may not know that it is against the law to harm, capture, or keep wild birds. It certainly is wrong as well.

Q: *I want to keep a nest of wild bunnies that I found. What should I feed them?*

Suffering in Silence. Injured by a blow dart, this pigeon doesn't appear to feel pain, but it does. (Critter Alley)

A: If you remove baby bunnies from their nest, they will probably die. Rabbits are terrified of people. They will do anything to get away from us—even break their backs smacking into cages, trying to hop away. Stress easily kills young wild bunnies that people capture. Even rehabilitators have difficulty raising them.

Instead of taking the bunnies, set a good example by leaving the nest alone, and tell others why they should do the same. Become a bunny expert, not a bunny-napper.

Q: *Are there places where people can volunteer directly with animals?*

A: There are wonderful volunteer opportunities in some rehabilitation centers. A lot depends on species that are being cared for. Marine mammals usually are too big and unpredictable for inexperienced volunteers or children to work with. On the other hand, some birds might be fine. If you are interested, contact rehabilitators in your area.

Q: *I want to work directly with wildlife. What careers should I plan for?*

A: People usually think of veterinarians when they consider wildlife careers, but there are other choices.

Blubbery Giant. *Marine mammal centers usually don't allow inexperienced or young people to volunteer directly with the animals because of the creatures' size. There are many other ways to help, though. (Caroline Brawner)*

Vet Tech. *Coleen Doucette, a wildlife rehabilitator, gives an education program with Beth, a broad-winged hawk. Doucette feels that her technical education has helped her work with wildlife and that her rehabilitation experience benefits her job as a vet tech in a veterinary clinic. (Coleen Doucette)*

Quite a few wildlife rehabilitators are veterinary technicians (vet techs). Vet techs are like animal care nurses. They often work in veterinary clinics, assisting veterinarians. To become a veterinary technician, a person typically attends two or three years of school at a junior college or training institute. Then he or she must pass a certification test in order to become licensed.

Why do so many vet techs become rehabilitators? A few admit that they want more challenges than working only with domestic animals. They believe that wildlife medicine is an exciting new frontier.

Other professionals who may work directly or indirectly with wildlife are those who specialize in biology, ecology, zoology, herpetology, or ornithology.

It is helpful to get as much volunteer experience as possible. This can include working at zoos, rehabilitation centers, nature centers, veterinary clinics, or wildlife parks. Also, check with organizations such as the Audubon Society or Sierra Club. They often offer field trips and other outdoor activities.

See the Resources section for other career information about working with wildlife.

Q: *I took twelve baby ducks home to raise. Now ten of them are dead. Will I get in trouble if I take the two living ducks to a rehabilitator?*

A: Call a wildlife rehabilitator or your state wildlife agency right away. The best chance for the ducklings is with a rehabilitator.

It's wonderful that you want to be close to wild creatures, but you do not need to take them home to enjoy them. Watch them in their wild world, where they will have the best chance to survive.

You will not get in trouble if you take the babies to a rehabilitator. But please learn from this sad mistake. Don't kidnap any more baby ducks. They need their mother's care. Mother ducks keep their babies warm and teach them important survival skills. Most humans do not know how to do that.

Q: *I like the names rehabbers give to animals. Does everyone do that?*

A: A few rehabbers do not name the animals because they worry about becoming too attached to the animals and having a hard time releasing them. Others name only animals used for purposes of education. Some give names to all the creatures, and what amazing imaginations they have! The animals do not know their names, of course. Rehabbers use names mainly to keep track of the many creatures they care for.

Susan Ahalt of Ironside Bird Rescue in Cody, Wyoming, even names *groups* of birds! And Cec and Tom Sanders love to play around with words while feeding deer in the "*doe*mitory" at the "or*fawn*age."

"The Fabulous Five." Susan Ahalt rehabilitated these orphaned kestrels after their nest tree was cut down. "Dent," the youngest (with taped wing), was released a few weeks after his siblings. (Susan Ahalt)

"The Dream Team." Susan Ahalt raised these five house wrens (as well as four barn swallows) and released them all back to the wild. (Bob Silva)

Quillma. (Tom Sanders)

KimBEARly. (Tom Sanders)

Dantelope and Diantelope. (Tom Sanders)

4

Release—The Last Step

Healed and Free. *Susan Ahalt of Ironside Bird Rescue in Cody, Wyoming, releases Piney Mack, a golden eagle she rehabilitated. With her are Dr. Bob Beiermann and his son, Clint. (B. D. Wehrfritz)*

Setting Wildlife Free

Wildlife cannot be turned loose just anywhere. The site has to be good for the animals and acceptable to nearby people.

Rehabbers start searching for release sites long before they free healthy wildlife. However, it is not easy to find good habitat with abundant food, water, shelter, and little contact with humans. Many habitats have been disrupted or destroyed by development.

Coleen Doucette of Acadia Wildlife Foundation in Mount Desert, Maine, lives on the border of Acadia National Park. It is an ideal place for releases.

"I'm lucky because I live up here in a corner of the country where we still have some wilderness left," Doucette said. "I have about two hundred acres of national park in my backyard, so I can open cage doors and let wildlife go."

At Big Sky Wildcare, a raptor rehabilitation center in Bozeman, Montana, volunteers started a Habitat Enhancement Program to create habitat for birds of prey and other wildlife. Volunteer experts in land-, bird-, water-, and habitat-related fields advise interested local landowners on how to manage their land to help wildlife. The land can range from a backyard to a big ranch.

If programs like this are successful, they will ensure that eagles and other raptors have quality habitat when they're released. Without good habitat, where will rehabilitated wildlife go?

Rare Room to Run. *A fox is released in Acadia National Park, which is Coleen Doucette's backyard. Good habitat is hard to find. (Coleen Doucette)*

Where Will Healed Eagles Go? *A Big Sky Wildcare volunteer releases a young bald eagle that was treated for poisoning. Without good habitat, recovered birds have no place to go. (Bobbi Geise)*

The Release Process

The release process starts when animals are moved to outdoor enclosures to live with others of their own species. They get used to weather conditions outside, and they receive less and less human attention. Enclosures may be located near forests or other habitats where the animals will be released. Some creatures even get visits from their future wild neighbors.

Slow Release. These young raccoons will receive food until they are able to survive on their own. (Critter Alley)

Before release, rehabilitators make sure the animals can fly, run, or climb normally. They also evaluate each animal's ability to see, hear, hunt or find natural foods, relate to its own species, and avoid enemies.

A release may be either slow or fast. In a slow release, the door of the pen or carrier is left open so the animal can come and go as it wants. The animal may be placed on a branch or in another safe place, away from predators. The rehabilitator keeps food at the release site until she knows that the animal is hunting or finding its own food. This type of release is a good approach for orphans.

In a fast release, the animal is taken to a release site, ideally one near where the animal was found, and let go. Fast releases are good for wilder creatures that don't need (or want) anything to do with people, especially animals that were admitted to the rehabilitation center as adults.

Sea Lion Release. Ken Lee (center) and other TMMC volunteers release rehabilitated sea lions on a beach. (© 1997 The Marine Mammal Center/Photo: Ken Bach)

Twilight. A gentle, trusting bird. (Lynne McCoy)

When a wild animal's injuries are too serious for recovery, the rehabilitator has to ask hard questions. Should the animal have to suffer in pain or forced captivity, or should it be euthanized? The decision is never easy, and rehabilitators agonize over the decision. But most of them would rather euthanize an animal than return it to the wild if it cannot survive on its own. In the wild it would suffer from slow starvation, or it would be hurt or killed by predators.

One unfortunate example was Twilight, a young red-tailed hawk that had been kept illegally. Neglected by his captor, Twilight suffered from blindness and other health problems caused by poor diet and improper care. Someone rescued Twilight and took him to Lynne McCoy, an independent rehabilitator in east Tennessee. McCoy paid special attention to the gentle bird, trying to make up for his losses.

When Twilight developed an infection in his head, McCoy took him to her veterinarian. An X-ray showed a lead pellet lodged in his brain where the hawk had been shot.

The infection got worse. When antibiotics and tender, loving care could not help anymore, McCoy gave Twilight the last kindness she could offer—euthanasia. Later, weeping as she penned a tribute to Twilight in her newsletter, McCoy wrote, "In my heart a redtail is soaring high, eyes bright, free of pain. Good-bye, Twilight."

In another case, the sheriff's department called Janet Walker (Critter Alley Wildlife Rehabilitation Center in Grand Ledge, Michigan) to report a raccoon limping along a highway. A steel-jawed

Caught. A raccoon in a leghold trap. (Critter Alley)

leghold trap was clamped to her paw. When Walker found her, the raccoon was curled up in shock; the trap had nearly cut off her paw. A nursing mother, she had tried to chew off the rest of her paw to get back to her babies.

Walker knew the raccoon's mangled paw would have to be amputated. She also knew that a raccoon's front paws are vital for its survival. They are used for finding food in water, prying open shellfish, feeding, walking, running, and climbing.

With a heavy heart, Walker decided to euthanize the raccoon rather than send her into a hopeless future. When the babies could not be found, Walker's heartache was doubled. She knew that the babies would die of starvation without their mother.

Frequently Asked Questions

Q: *Do rehabilitators ever get bitten or scratched by the animals they treat?*

A: Most rehabilitators probably would admit to being bitten, scratched, or jabbed a few times. After all, helpless animals have to defend themselves the best way they can—with teeth, claws, and beaks. A part of training to become a rehabilitator involves learning how to properly handle wild creatures. This skill protects animals *and* people.

Don't Badger Me! Learning how to safely handle all kinds of creatures is an important part of wildlife rehabilitation. (Shannon K. Jacobs)

Q: *Why do rehabilitators euthanize animals? Aren't they supposed to save, not kill, them?*

A: The goal of rehabilitation is to help sick, orphaned, or injured wildlife recover and return to the wild. Unfortunately, not all animals recover. About half of the animals admitted to rehabilitation centers cannot be released. They are either too badly injured or too sick. Some of these creatures live in constant pain. Others have lost their eyesight, legs, wings, or beaks. They cannot eat, fly, or walk.

Should these animals be confined to cages, forever yearning to be free? Do they have a right to be released from pain and suffering? In the wild they would go hungry, or predators (including people) would hurt or kill them.

Permit requirements do not allow rehabilitators to keep unreleasable animals unless they are used for education (which requires other special permits). Even if they could keep them, how could rehabilitators possibly pay for the care of hundreds of thousands of hopelessly sick or injured wild animals? With so little money available to treat wildlife, isn't that money better spent on animals that are able to survive in the wild?

Choosing to euthanize an animal is a very painful decision. Some rehabbers cry their eyes out, and it never gets easier for them. The only thing that helps is knowing that they have released the animal from a life of misery.

What about the people who harmed the animals in the first place—what responsibility do they have in the suffering and death of wildlife? What can we all do to prevent wildlife injuries so these painful decisions do not have to be made?

Q: *How many rehabilitated animals are released?*

A: Generally, fewer than half the animals admitted to a rehabilitation center are released. That may not sound like very many, but remember that quite a few of these animals are severely injured or dangerously sick when admitted.

Adopted Bird Visit. *Jacki Wallace, a volunteer with Birds of Prey Foundation, holds Chaco (a Swainson's hawk), an education bird. Chaco was adopted by this sixth-grade class. (Shannon K. Jacobs)*

What happens to the animals that are not released? Most of them die or are euthanized. A few are kept as permanent education animals or transferred to other centers, museums, or zoos for displays or for captive breeding.

Q: *How can people help rehabilitators?*

1. Donate money. Rehabilitators always need help with expenses.
2. Ask rehabilitators if they have a wish list of items they need, from animal foods and paper towels to computers and vehicles.
3. Become a volunteer. You may be the perfect person to help build or clean cages, feed and rescue animals, answer phones, or help with fund-raising.
4. Join a local wildlife rehabilitation organization. Basic memberships vary from $10 to $25 a year. Usually you receive a newsletter published by the center. Newsletters feature fascinating information: rescue tips, information about various animals, and stories about the critters cared for at the center. You, your family, or a classroom can "adopt" an animal if you donate money at a certain level to help pay for its care. A photo of the animal may be sent to you, or you may be able to name it. Some centers let adoptive parents help with the animal's release. If it is an education animal, a class involved in its adoption might receive a special visit.
5. Ask for a really wild birthday present. Send family and friends the name and address of your favorite wildlife rehabilitation center. Ask them to make a donation, take out a membership, or sponsor an adoption in your name. It's a great gift for everyone!
6. Tell others about rehabilitators.
7. Learn how to prevent wildlife injuries (see Chapter 9).
8. Don't be a baby-napper (see Chapters 2, 3, and 9).

Wildlife Hero. *For two and a half years, thirteen-year-old Mark July has spent his Sundays volunteering at Critter Alley Wildlife Rehabilitation Center in Michigan. (Critter Alley)*

5

Learning More About Wildlife

Ready for School. *Susan Ahalt of Ironside Bird Rescue in Cody, Wyoming, and Snap, a great horned owl and an education bird, pause before giving a school presentation. (Rosemary Perfit)*

Sharing the Wonder

Teaching people about wildlife is very important to rehabilitators. They answer countless questions over the phone, teach anyone who brings them an animal, and give thousands of structured education programs a year. All these methods of education help children and adults learn about wildlife habitats and native animals, endangered species, peaceful ways to live with wildlife, and ways to protect wild creatures.

Exciting School Programs: Bat Woman

When Penny Murphy of Urban Wildlife Rescue in Aurora, Colorado, visits schools, she shows fantastic slides of bats. She also passes around a few stuffed bats that died from their injuries. During Murphy's programs, students learn about the importance of bats, ways to protect them, and why they should never touch bats on the ground. Even children who enter the room afraid of bats soon become batty for the furry, flying mammals.

Safe School Bats. Penny Murphy takes stuffed bats to schools during her education programs, so kids can touch them safely. (Notice the bat sticker on her cheek?) (Shannon K. Jacobs)

Nonreleasable Animals

Some rehabilitators hold education permits that allow them to keep nonreleasable wild animals for use in education programs. (These permits do *not* allow animals being rehabilitated for release to be used for education.)

Nonreleasable animals are those with permanent injuries that would prevent them from surviving in the wild. For example, some birds can survive with only one eye or one leg. But if part of a wing is missing, they will not be able to fly or hunt. Many birds that are human-imprinted cannot be released.

Education animals are great teachers. School classes consider it quite an honor to get a visit from an eagle, turtle, snake, or opossum. However, just because an animal cannot be released doesn't mean it likes to be around people. Education animals have to be trained to tolerate noisy crowds. Those that never learn to accept humans cannot be used in education programs.

Diane Johnson of Operation WildLife (OWL) in Linwood, Kansas, takes education raptors to many schools. Before she takes the birds into a public setting, however, she trains them several hours a day for six to twelve months. How does she train raptors to put up with people? She described it as a "long process with a lot of repetition." At night, after her three children are asleep, Johnson grabs a book and sits down next to a new eagle or hawk in its cage. She reads aloud for a few hours at a time, letting the bird get used to her voice. When the bird has learned to tolerate her, Johnson slowly begins to introduce it to other people.

Squirrelly Teacher. *Megan, a squirrel blinded by pesticide spray, visited many classrooms in east Tennessee with rehabilitator Lynne McCoy. (Lynne McCoy)*

At Liberty Wildlife Rehabilitation Foundation in Scottsdale, Arizona, thirty raptors are kept as education birds. "Manning" (training) the new education birds is a slow and respectful process, according to volunteer educator Anne Steinmetz.

Each day the birds are fed (some by hand) in the same place at the same time so they know what to expect from their human caretakers. The

Fairy Tale Tonight? *Diane Johnson reads aloud to new education animals, such as this bald eagle, to allow them to adjust to people slowly. (KDWP)*

birds slowly get used to wearing jesses (leather leg straps), which allow trainers to catch the birds without having to grab bodies or wings and possibly injure the birds. The trainers can then teach the birds to step up and stand on a glove. When the birds are comfortable on a glove, they begin meeting other people.

From October through May, the education birds at Liberty Wildlife travel to many schools and community centers around the Phoenix area. They teach people the rapture of raptors. In June, off come those jesses. Like other hardworking teachers, Liberty Wildlife birds deserve their summers off!

Arranging Education Visits

If a class would like a visit from a rehabilitator with education animals, the teacher should get a list of nearby wildlife rehabilitators with education permits. The teacher can call the state wildlife agency for information.

Respectful Group. Preschoolers listen to Birds of Prey Foundation volunteer Jacki Wallace talk about Spud, a screech owl education bird. (Shannon K. Jacobs)

If a class schedules a program with a wildlife rehabilitator and an education animal, the teacher might want to discuss ahead of time how students can behave quietly and respectfully in the animal's presence.

Some centers, especially large ones, will let individuals or school groups tour part of the facilities. Others may not have enough room to separate the sick animals from crowds of people, so they do not allow visits. Since their main purpose is to care for wildlife, rehabilitators have to weigh the advantages of letting people visit the center.

Even if you are able to tour a center, you probably will not be able to see all the animals. Those that are being rehabilitated for release should never be disturbed by the public. It is very important that visitors respect this policy. The animals become very stressed if they see or hear humans. They need to stay as wild as possible so they will be able to survive when released.

A few centers have one-way glass in front of enclosures, so visitors can watch the animals without the animals seeing them. This is an ideal way for the public to experience and appreciate the incredible work of rehabilitators. Unfortunately, it is very expensive, and most centers cannot afford it.

Improving Wildlife Treatment

Research

In order to manage wildlife properly, scientists and biologists need to learn as much as possible about the animals. Because it is often difficult to study animals in the wild, rehabilitation centers provide excellent opportunities to investigate wild creatures in temporary captivity.

In some centers scientists are researching treatments for wildlife diseases, lead poisoning, and oil soaking. Other research focuses on learning more about specific animals or endangered species.

Bat Courtship

As the only volunteer rehabilitator at Bat World Sanctuary (Mineral Wells, Texas), Amanda Lollar has spent more than fifteen thousand hours with a colony of fifty Mexican free-tailed bats. Lollar observes the bats closely while hand-feeding them. Because they are used to her, the bats behave naturally. This has allowed Lollar to witness free-tail courting and mating behavior that has never been seen before.

Mexican Free-Tailed Bat. *Amanda Lollar's observations of a captive colony of free-tails may help save the species, which is declining in the wild. (Amanda Lollar)*

Lollar also has recorded free-tail courting songs. These sounds may help biologists identify key caves in the wild where free-tails breed. If the caves can be protected, this will be an important step in saving Mexican free-tails. Their numbers are declining at an alarming rate because of habitat loss.

What Do Manatees Hear?

Can manatees hear motorboats coming toward them in time to get away? A researcher at the David A. Straz, Jr., Manatee Hospital (Lowry Park Zoo in Tampa, Florida) has studied the hearing of manatees, hoping to answer that question. The researcher discovered the bad news that manatees cannot hear motorboats because their hearing frequency is different from that of humans. The good news, however, is that we now know what manatees *can* hear, so new research can focus on developing manatee-warning devices within the animals' hearing range. Because endangered manatees are regularly injured and killed by speed boats, such research will help protect these gentle mammals.

Postrelease Studies

Many centers find out what happens to their rehabilitated animals by tracking them through radio transmitters. Such post-release studies tell rehabilitators where their former patients go and how they adjust to the wild. This is particularly important when large predators, such as cougars and bears, are released. Wildlife officials want to be sure they are staying far away from people.

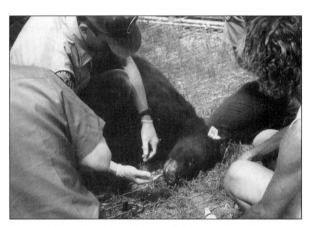

Collaring Black Bears. State wildlife officials tranquilized this rehabilitated black bear orphan and fit a radio collar around his neck. Once released, the bear can be tracked for follow-up. (Tom Sanders)

Following Black Bears

Cec and Tom Sanders (Wet Mountain Wildlife Rehabilitation in Florence, Colorado) have cared for more than one hundred young black bears over the past twenty-five years. The Colorado Division of Wildlife radio-collared and tracked several of the bears after they were released.

"The bears did fine," Cec Sanders said. "Wildlife officials are finding that cubs seem to stay put when they are relocated after rehab. The cubs don't try to return. Maybe that's because they don't have a territory yet."

That behavior is very important in states such as Colorado that have a "two strikes and you're dead" policy for bears. A bear that is considered a problem because it has had conflicts with people is ear-tagged and relocated to wilderness areas twice. If it returns or gets in trouble after that, the bear is killed.

Wired for Release. Two harbor seal pups wear radio transmitters glued to their fur. (© 1997 The Marine Mammal Center/Photo: Jane Oka)

Tracking Seals

For several years, The Marine Mammal Center in Sausalito, California, has tracked orphaned harbor seals after release, and researchers have learned a lot about how seals manage on their own. Tiny radio transmitters are carefully glued to fur on the back of the seals' heads, and researchers follow the animals' activities for three to six months. When the seals molt, the transmitters fall off.

Medical and Surgical Advances

Sometimes wild animals benefit from treatments for domestic animals. A dramatic example is Helmethead, a red-tailed hawk that made medical history in Morgan Hill, California.

Helmethead was rescued by Sue Howell, director of Wildlife Education and Rehabilitation Center (W.E.R.C.). The hawk suffered from a head injury, infected scalp, and missing head feathers. Howell took the hawk to Dr. John Quick of the Animal Medical Clinic, who ordered medicated bandages for the restless raptor's head. To keep the dressings in place, Howell designed a special hat that looked like a helmet (hence the hawk's name). During the next year of recovery, Helmethead's infection cleared up, and the bird became stronger. But she still had a serious

Missing: Head Feathers. Helmethead, an injured red-tailed hawk, waits for surgery. (W.E.R.C.)

problem—no scalp feathers. Birds need all their feathers in perfect condition in order to fly and to stay warm and dry. Even a few missing head feathers can affect their ability to survive.

The veterinarian decided to do a sliding skin-graft surgery on the bald hawk. Although this surgery had been performed before on cats and dogs, it had never been done on birds. The procedure involved cutting some of the

hawk's neck skin (with feathers) and stretching the skin over her head. When Helmethead woke up from the surgery, she had a fringe of neck feathers on the back of her head. More feathers were expected to grow in time.

The hawk recovered quickly, and everyone at W.E.R.C. and the clinic celebrated when she was

Getting Stronger. A newly feathered Helmethead strengthens her wings, preparing for freedom. (W.E.R.C.)

Oiled Bird. *An Atlantic puffin was wrapped in a bootie (operating room paper slipper) to keep the bird from preening (cleaning itself) and swallowing oil. (Karen Von den Deale)*

Clean as a Whistle. *After receiving successful oiled-bird treatment at Wild Care, Inc., the puffin was released. (Karen Von den Deale)*

released a few months later. The best news of all came when someone spotted Helmethead a year and a half later, still going strong.

Oil Spills

For many years wildlife rehabilitators have contributed vital help during oil spills. In 1989 they quickly responded to the *Exxon Valdez* oil spill in Alaska. This spill, the worst in U.S. history, happened when a supertanker ran aground, dumping eleven million gallons of crude oil into Prince William Sound. That day the waters of the sound were filled with marine animals, seabirds, and flocks of migrating birds. Thousands of animals died immediately from the toxic effects of the spreading oil, and many others became very sick.

Oil destroys the waterproofing and insulating properties of feathers and fur. If not treated immediately, oiled animals die from cold, starvation, pneumonia, or kidney disease. In their weakened condition, they are helpless against predators. The predators also become poisoned by the oil if they eat oiled prey.

Oiled-animal rehabilitation is a specialized treatment that should be done by or supervised by wildlife rehabilitators who are specially trained in oiled-animal care. Untrained people may not understand that oil is toxic and therefore dangerous if they inhale fumes or get it on their skin. Also, experienced rehabilitators know how to protect animals from the deadly effects of stress during capture, treatment, and release. Most oiled animals can't eat because they're too sick, so rehabilitators have to tube-feed them or give them fluids and medications intravenously. When the animals' conditions become stable, volunteers begin the long, hard job of washing oil out of fur and feathers.

Wildlife rehabilitators saved hundreds of birds and mammals in Prince William Sound, a project that took enormous skill, expense, and teamwork. The knowledge gained from treating so many animals at once was invaluable for the future because every year there are hundreds of oil spills in U.S. waters.

Some rehab centers have formed their own oil-response teams. They share the knowledge they gain with other wildlife people, teaching them the most effective and up-to-date methods in caring for oiled animals.

For more information about oiled wildlife, check out these websites and their links:

International Bird Rescue Research Center: www.ibrrc.org

Tri-State Bird Rescue and Research: www.tristatebird.org

Oiled Wildlife Care Network: www.vetmed.ucdavis.edu/owcn/

The Marine Mammal Center: www.tmmc.org

Most oiled animals do not survive, even with the skill and courageous efforts of many volunteers trying to save them. Hence, prevention of oil spills is the most important way to avoid the tragedies of oiled wildlife.

6
Rehabilitating Mammals and Reptiles

Fawn Therapy. *Janet Walker, director of Critter Alley Wildlife Rehabilitation Center in Grand Ledge, Michigan, gives physical therapy to a fawn with an injured leg. (Critter Alley)*

Night Prowler. *Skunks are nocturnal animals. (Critter Alley)*

Even in big cities, wild animals share our space. You may never see them, but all kinds of nocturnal creatures (such as raccoons, opossums, foxes, coyotes, skunks, and bats) prowl around in the dark. Other creatures—snakes, squirrels, groundhogs, turtles, and bears—are more noticeable because they are diurnal. A few, such as deer and rabbits, are crepuscular (mostly active at dusk and dawn).

Like birds and sea mammals, land animals are completely dependent on their habitat for survival, relying on very specific wild foods and dwellings. When wildlife homes are destroyed, some animals are killed instantly; others are driven away. Rehabilitators receive some of these displaced animals, along with the huge challenge of finding decent habitat for release.

Hibernation

Hibernation helps animals such as groundhogs, chipmunks, ground squirrels, and marmots survive when food sources are not available. During hibernation, the breathing and heart rate slow down, and the body temperature drops a few degrees. These changes help to conserve energy so animals can survive the winter with little or no food.

How does hibernation affect rehabilitation? It can influence when an animal is released. For example, if it is October, and a groundhog is ready for release but doesn't have enough body fat to survive four to six months without eating, the animal cannot be returned to the wild.

Animals prepare for hibernation by wolfing down enormous amounts of food, starting in late summer. They have to put on enough body fat to last through the winter. If injured animals are still recovering, and it is close to hibernation time, rehabbers may "winter" them at the center to allow their healing processes to continue.

Rabies

Another consideration in working with land animals is the threat of rabies. In some states rehabbers are not allowed to work with bats, skunks, coyotes, raccoons, or foxes because they are vector species—the most likely to get rabies and infect other animals. Some states require rehabilitators to take special training classes to learn how to safely handle rabies vector species and to prevent the spread of diseases. Most rehabbers protect themselves by being vaccinated against rabies. Then, if they are bit or scratched by a rabid animal, they will need just booster shots.

Reptiles

Unlike mammals, reptiles do not maintain a steady body temperature. They rely on their surroundings to warm them up and cool them off. Because of these temperature needs, reptiles live in very specific places.

Releasing rehabilitated reptiles back to the wild must be done carefully. Some reptiles live in tiny territories, and if they are removed from that territory and released somewhere else, they may not be able to reproduce or survive. Sometimes turtles that are moved from a territory being developed will return to that area when released and may end up crushed by bulldozers.

Gila Monster. This poisonous reptile, stolen from the wild and kept as a "pet," cannot be released because it might be carrying diseases that could wipe out a wild population. (Shannon K. Jacobs)

Captive reptiles pick up diseases easily. If released, they may spread the diseases to wild, endangered populations, which is one reason why people who are not rehabilitators should never turn animals loose into the wild. Only wildlife rehabilitators or state wildlife officials should make such decisions.

Lynne McCoy

Location: 630 Crestfield Drive
New Market, TN 37820
865-397-9540
E-mail: backwoodslynne@aol.com

Description: Independent rehabilitator, treating 250 to 350 small mammals, birds, and reptiles a year

Staff: McCoy (licensed) and volunteers

Funding: Accepts donations; mostly funded by McCoy; this is *not* a nonprofit center.

Newsletter: *It's a WildLife*, published 4 times a year

Programs: 10–20 school and community education programs annually

Tours: No

Joy of Release. Lynne McCoy sets free a healed red-tailed hawk, Remington. The bird had been shot in the wing. (David McCoy)

For more than thirty years, Lynne McCoy has cared for many colorful creatures with the help of her husband, David, and other volunteers. She also advises hundreds of people over the phone about wildlife issues.

McCoy works closely with Dr. Stephen Burns, a local veterinarian who enjoys using his skills to help wildlife.

"What keeps me going," McCoy said, "is seeing a bird fly free, a squirrel go up a tree, or an opossum waddle off after I helped it over the bad times. I like knowing an animal is back where it belongs.

"Sometimes injured animals just need time to rest and heal," she explained. "In the wild, they don't get that. When they're helpless, they get nailed fast."

Somehow McCoy finds the time to publish a wildly entertaining newsletter, *It's a WildLife*, four times a year. Each issue is filled with true stories, fascinating facts, and helpful hints about the wildlife McCoy helps. Always enjoying a laugh, she generously sprinkles the newsletters with her wonderful sense of humor.

Jake the Entertainer

When giving school programs, McCoy likes to take education animals with her. One animal that often stole the spotlight was Jake, the opossum. Jake was the first opossum many students had ever seen up close. And what an impression he made! Before each program, Jake would wrap his tail around McCoy's wrist for extra support before meeting his loud, adoring fans.

Crow Attack. Dr. Stephen Burns examines a great horned owl that was knocked out of a tree by crows. *(Lynne McCoy)*

Jake enjoyed showing off his table manners by spoon-feeding himself, a skill he had learned while recovering from a broken jaw he suffered after getting hit by a car. McCoy had spoon-fed the opossum for several weeks.

In his short lifetime Jake entertained, educated, and inspired thousands of children and adults. The finest tribute paid to this gentle marsupial was when a former elementary student said to McCoy, "Because of Jake, I check the pouches of all road-killed opossums, just in case there are babies to save!" Jake would have been proud. He died in his sleep as peacefully as he had lived.

Jake the Opossum. Unreleasable because of permanent injuries, Jake was an education animal who loved to show off his manners for schoolkids. *(Lynne McCoy)*

Whistler's Mother?

Whistledigger was hairless and the size of a thumb when a dog snatched her. Luckily, the dog was a retriever and knew how to carry his mouthful home tenderly, causing just minor bite wounds. The only problem was, nobody knew what the dog had brought home!

A veterinary clinic asked if McCoy would care for the mystery animal, so she said yes and examined the creature. She knew it was a rodent, but what

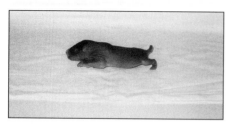

Mystery. What did the dog bring home? (Lynne McCoy)

Grown-up Groundhog. Whistledigger filled out fast and soon was returned to the wild. (Lynne McCoy)

kind? After ruling out what it was *not*, McCoy figured out what it *was*.

"Groundhog!" she announced.

Groundhogs are normally well developed by the time they leave their burrows. So where had this baby come from? McCoy thought she may have been dropped by her mother or flooded out of her home.

McCoy named the groundhog Whistledigger because she whistled when she wanted attention. Groundhogs make several sounds, including high-pitched whistles.

Did that make McCoy "Whistler's Mother"? asked her husband, David.

Whistledigger grew up quickly. Soon McCoy released the fat, healthy, and feisty groundhog back to the wild.

Summer of the Rowdy Raccoons

When they admitted four baby raccoons at one time, Lynne and David McCoy geared themselves up for a wild and crazy summer. They were not disappointed.

The first to arrive was Rikki, chittering and purring. He was the only raccoon in his family to survive when his nest tree was cut down. Next came Rachel, who had been found along a highway. McCoy figured Rachel's mother had accidentally dropped the furry bundle while moving her.

Two other baby coons, Rocket and Racket, a brother and sister, were found starving in the woods. They were so young that their eyes were still closed. (Raccoon babies open their eyes about the third week of life.)

The McCoys raised the four baby raccoons together, feeding them, keeping them warm, and laughing at their funny tricks and treats. When the youngsters grew into restless teenagers, McCoy took them to another rehabilitation center that had a big outdoor cage. Although she knew it was time to leave the young animals, McCoy had a hard time letting them go. She said that walking away from those young raccoons was one of the hardest things she had ever done.

Something to Think About

Rehabilitators understand why people want to keep wild babies as pets. But they also know what kind of future awaits a "tame" wild animal. In her newsletter, McCoy described why wild ones do not make good pets:

> "Gee this baby squirrel is cute, and so is the baby raccoon, and I just know they'll make wonderful pets." WRONG.
>
> Those cute babies grow up, and cute habits aren't so cute anymore. Wrestling with the little squirrel and raccoon ... soon the squirrel bites, and those teeth are like chisels.
>
> The little coon weighs 20 pounds, and wrestling isn't such fun anymore, but the coon doesn't know why you won't play. He's bored so he destroys the house or bites (they bite when they can't have their way) and won't accept discipline. He tears up his cage.
>
> But he's been fed candy and is people-oriented, and now has cataracts (cloudy lens of the eyes caused from malnutrition), and the squirrel has chewed through the phone wire. Or, even worse, the raccoon has been declawed to protect the furniture.
>
> Now you don't want them anymore ... but no zoo will accept them, no one else wants them for pets ... so you turn them loose ... and they die in miserable ways—attacks from other animals, slow starvation, or going up to strangers and acting friendly and getting shot or beaten to death.
>
> **But in reality, these animals were as good as dead the day you decided to keep them as pets.**

A Four-Coon Night. *Rikki, Rachel, Rocket, and Racket keep each other company. (Lynne McCoy)*

When Cute Babies Get Big. *Don't steal babies from the wild to keep as pets. They are dangerous and unmanageable as adults, and no one wants them then. (Urban Wildlife Rescue)*

Bat World Sanctuary

Location: 217 N. Oak Avenue
Mineral Wells, TX 76067
940-325-3404
www.batworld.org
E-mail: sanctuary@batworld.org

Description: Bat rehabilitation center (about 1,000 bats rehabbed per year) and lifetime sanctuary for nonreleasable bats

Staff: 1 volunteer rehabilitator

Funding: Education programs, private donations, newsletter subscriptions

Newsletter: *Bat World News*, published quarterly

Programs: Field trips, guided tours for school and civic groups, "Bat Chat" assemblies at north-central Texas schools

Tours: Yes, with admission donation and by reservation; open every second Saturday and third Sunday of the month, September–May (check website)

In 1994 Amanda Lollar sold her furniture business and got the proper permits to start Bat World, a sanctuary and educational center for bats. It's also a permanent home for one hundred nonreleasable bats.

Most of the permanent residents have been confiscated from illegal pet traders, used in research, orphaned, or permanently injured. A large colony of Mexican free-tailed bats are among them.

The Enchanted Forest. Amanda Lollar gives students a tour of the rainforest habitat she built for the one hundred–plus resident bats at Bat World. Visitors can see bats, such as Bucko (upper right), up close, but they can't touch them. (Luanne Albright)

When schools or community groups take field trips to Bat World, visitors can walk through Lollar's miniature Enchanted Forest, where they can see ten different species of bats in natural-habitat flight cages.

Sunshine

Although she is dedicated to educating others about the wonder of bats, Lollar understands people's fears about them. She used to consider bats "vermin" too. But that was before she met Sunshine.

In 1988, Lollar found an injured Mexican free-tailed bat lying on a hot downtown sidewalk. Taking pity on the poor creature, Lollar moved it into shade. She wanted the bat to be able to die in peace. But when the bat didn't die, Lollar took it home, then hurried to the library to read up on bats. Her reading showed her how fascinating and helpful the furry animals are. Lollar named the Mexican free-tail Sunshine and took care of her until the little bat died two years later. In 1991 Lollar wrote *The Bat in My*

Sunshine II. Amanda Lollar cared for this Mexican free-tail after Sunshine died. (Amanda Lollar)

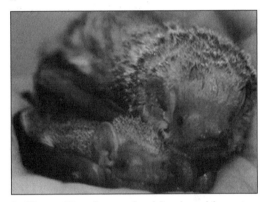

Red Bat and Pup. Someone found these bats while mowing his lawn. Mom and baby were treated and released. Lollar reminds people, especially kids, "Never touch a bat." (Amanda Lollar)

Pocket, a beautiful book about her close relationship with Sunshine. Many people who read the book say they will never feel the same way about bats again.

Lollar is a licensed rehabilitator who has been vaccinated against rabies. She frequently reminds people—especially children—to *never touch a bat*. Although most bats are not diseased, no one should take a chance.

Lollar puts in long days at Bat World. Just taking care of nonreleasable bats takes six to eight hours a day. She rehabilitates orphaned, sick, and injured bats in a separate room. Lollar has rehabilitated and released thousands of bats, which has been good news for Mineral Wells's mosquito control. Just one Mexican free-tailed bat (Texas's most common species) can eat three thousand to five thousand insects a night!

Bat Chats

Lollar takes four species of bats with her when she gives "Bat Chat" assembly programs in north-central Texas schools. Students are able to see (but not touch) small insect-eating bats and large fruit bats up close and on a TV screen. They learn the importance of leaving wild bats alone, and they find out the proper steps to take if they find sick or injured bats.

"After spending thousands of hours watching bats with their gentle, intelligent ways, it's impossible to imagine my life without them," Lollar said. "In many ways they are cleaner and nicer to each other than people are.

"My greatest reward is helping people change their minds about bats. There's no way anyone could see normal bats up close and walk away feeling bad about them."

Bucko the Klutzy Bat

"The Amazing Bucko" is a favorite attraction for kids visiting Bat World. A bucktoothed African straw-colored flying fox, Bucko likes to stretch out his wings and show off his three-foot wingspan. He was donated by Bat Conser-

Bucko the Bully. An African straw-colored flying fox bat, Bucko (right), hangs out with his much smaller fruit bat friends. (Amanda Lollar)

vation International (BCI), a well-known organization that researches and protects bats.

"Bucko's so incredibly goofy," Lollar said. "He tries to get into the little fruit bats' roosts for no reason at all, other than the little bats are in there."

The roosts are little wicker baskets that hang upside down. Bucko is a foot long, and the Jamaican fruit bats are only a third his size. So Bucko throws his weight around, swatting at the smaller bats until they leave their baskets. Then he climbs inside their roosts.

"He's such a clown," Lollar said. "Three-fourths of his body hangs out of their baskets."

As payback, the little Jamaican fruit bats go by and swat Bucko's bell, a bird bell hanging in the rainforest flight cage. When Bucko hears them whacking his bell, he shrieks and flies off to defend his territory.

Puttering Around

When Lollar found Putter, an orphaned Mexican free-tail, the little bat was only an inch long, hairless, and full of mites.

"Her legs were clamped up next to her body, and her knees were stiff as a board," Lollar said. "I figured she'd been born breech because breech free-tails have a problem with their legs."

Lollar cleaned up the infant bat, made braces for her, and began physical therapy on her legs. While brushing Putter's fur, Lollar noticed that the bat's legs jerked reflexively, like a dog's, so brushing then became part of the therapy to build up Putter's weak leg muscles. Now Putter can move around fairly well, hang upside down, and groom herself all over. She is not strong enough to be released, but because she is used to people and bright lights, Putter will become an education animal. Soon she'll visit schools and other places, helping more people learn about the beauty and benefits of bats.

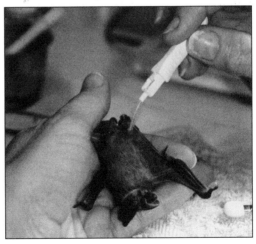

Kicking Therapy. When Lollar brushes Putter's fur, the little bat kicks like a dog. (Amanda Lollar)

Greenwood Wildlife Rehabilitation Sanctuary

Location: PO Box 18987
Boulder, CO 80308
303-545-5849
www.greenwoodwildlife.org
E-mail: greenwood@estreet.com

Description: Large center treating more than 3,500 small mammals, birds, and reptiles a year

Staff: 2 paid staff, more than 125 volunteers

Funding: Donations, memberships, fund-raisers

Newsletter: *Pinecoon Press,* published 2–4 times a year

Programs: Many, including interactive picture boards, slide shows, mystery mammal games, portable hospital, and displays

Tours: Only during open house, held every spring

Greenwood was named after the sanctuary's first patient, a severely burned raccoon. He was rescued from a chimney fire, rehabilitated, and released.

Other creatures treated at Greenwood include orphaned and adult coyotes, bats, foxes, squirrels, prairie dogs, turtles, and snakes. Many species of land and water birds also are rehabilitated.

Volunteers answer phones, clean cages, chop up food, feed babies, rescue and transport animals, and raise money. In one year, they handled more than five thousand hotline calls. Many veterinarians also donate their services, examining and treating sick and injured animals.

Volunteer Rehabilitators. Ellen Schultz (left) and Jan Bova (right) examine a newly admitted sparrow nestling found under a tree. (Shannon K. Jacobs)

Greenwood's newsletter, *Pinecoon Press,* features photos and stories about rescues, treatments, and releases. A special column called "Whatever Happened to … ?" updates readers on animals described in other issues.

Wildly Popular Programs

Greenwood's education programs reach more than two thousand people a year. They are especially popular with elementary and middle school students. Imagine a whole class of seventh graders wildly waving their hands in the air, begging to participate in a program—that's what happened when Ellen Schultz, education coordinator, wheeled her portable hospital and stuffed staff into Broomfield Heights Middle School. Schultz selected a few lucky volunteers to treat the wild animals she had brought with her. They were stuffed animals, naturally, but their injuries were based on real cases treated at the sanctuary. The students learned how to bottle-feed (and burp) raccoon babies, give antibiotic injections to a snake, rescue a prairie dog stuck in a six-pack ring, and help a coyote with a broken leg.

Later, looking like raccoon kits feeling everything with their paws, the eager seventh graders handled the fascinating display pieces Schultz had set out. They included real beaks, talons, skulls, feathers, shells, stuffed bats, and birds' nests. Greenwood has special government permits allowing it to keep these animal parts for education programs.

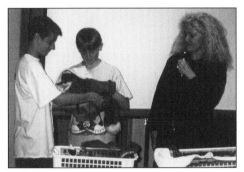

Lucky Volunteers. *Using a stuffed fox as model, Ellen Schultz (right) instructs seventh graders David Fredericks (left) and Shawn Hansen (middle) on how rehabilitators would treat a real injured fox. Greenwood's "Portable Hospital and Stuffed Staff" presentations are a big hit at schools. (Shannon K. Jacobs)*

Displaced Coyote. *DIA (named for Denver International Airport) was rescued as a pup after his burrow was bulldozed during construction of a new airport. DIA was rehabilitated at Greenwood and released, a very wily coyote. (Greenwood Wildlife Rehabilitation Sanctuary)*

Humpty Dumpty

First a car ran over Tex, a western box turtle, and crushed his shell. Then flies laid eggs in the cracks. By the time Tex arrived at Greenwood, hundreds of maggots were feeding on the turtle's infected flesh. For days rehabilitators picked off the maggots, flushed the infected skin, and gave Tex injections of antibiotics. Slowly the turtle's skin began to heal. A veterinarian used dental acrylic to patch cracks in the turtle's shell. Dental acrylic acts like Super Glue,

How Tex Got His Name. The white dental acrylic patch is shaped like the state of Texas. (Can you guess which state the veterinarian who glued Tex back together again is from?) (Greenwood Wildlife Rehabilitation Sanctuary)

keeping the shell in one piece until the damaged tissue can regenerate on its own.

So, unlike Humpty Dumpty, Tex *was* put back together again. But rehabilitators weren't through with him yet—the next step was to stop him from hibernating. If Tex snoozed through the winter, his body processes, including the healing of his shell, would slow down. Rehabilitators kept Tex warm all winter and fooled the turtle's body into thinking it was summer.

While their human caretakers shivered in snow and ice, Tex and his girl-friend, Painter, lounged around in light and warmth, nibbling melon chunks, carrots, and earthworms, and waited for spring.

Peanut Pinkies

While trimming a tree, a man found a nest of newborn squirrels inside a cut-off limb. His wife kept the babies warm and took them to Greenwood. New-born squirrels are called "pinkies" because they are pink, hairless, and helpless. They are born with eyes and ears closed, and they cannot control their body temperature or functions. Without a mother, babies this young (they were two days old) cannot survive.

Karen Taylor, animal care coordinator at Greenwood, became the pinkies' foster mother. During the day she took the tiny babies to the sanctuary with

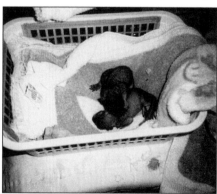

Growing Coats. These pinky squirrels are starting to grow fur. (Greenwood Wildlife Rehabilitation Sanctuary)

her. At night, Taylor kept them at her home, feeding them every two hours around the clock. They slept in a warm basket.

Two and a half weeks later, the little male died, in spite of all that Taylor did to save him. The females did well, though. When their fur started growing in, Taylor named them Slick (because of the slicked-back fur on her head) and Kinky (because her tail fur grew in kinks).

When Kinky and Slick got older, Taylor put them in with another squirrel named

Twinkie, the victim of a cat attack. The three squirrels raced, leaped, and climbed around the cage like furry little gymnasts. During one spectacular jump, Slick broke her rear foot. Taylor rushed her to the veterinarian for X-rays, worried because hind feet are very important for squirrels' survival: they are needed for climbing trees and escaping enemies. But Slick recovered well after wearing a tiny cast for a while and getting a lot of rest. By the time the scampering squirrels were moved to a bigger outdoor cage, their bodies were covered with thick fur. Wild as the wind, the young rodents did not want anything to do with humans, but that did not hurt Taylor's feelings. It meant that she and other Greenwood rehabilitators had done an excellent job of keeping the wild rodents wild. The proud foster mom released the three squirrels later.

Orphaned Fox Kit.
(Greenwood Wildlife Rehabilitation Sanctuary)

Fox Release. *(Greenwood Wildlife Rehabilitation Sanctuary)*

Outa Here!
(Greenwood Wildlife Rehabilitation Sanctuary)

Critter Alley Wildlife Rehabilitation Center

Critter Alley Wildlife Rehabilitation Center was started in 1988 in Grand Ledge, Michigan. Unfortunately, it closed in 2002. The following background and stories about its devoted staff, supportive public, and wildlife patients are still relevant today.

When Janet Walker was twelve years old, she found a rabbit that had been bitten by a dog. Even the sight of maggots squirming inside the rabbit's open wounds did not stop her from helping the poor creature heal and return to its wild home. That was more than forty years ago. From 1988 to 2002, Walker was director of Critter Alley Wildlife Rehabilitation Center, located on an eight-acre farm that she owned.

Among volunteers donating their time at the center were young people involved in the Junior Volunteer Program. Headed by two long-term volunteers, the juniors fed and cleaned the adult animals, groomed and exercised education animals, warmed bottles, and cleaned nursery incubators.

Junior volunteers also helped with fund-raising—a very important activity including aluminum-can drives, T-shirt sales, education programs, and Bingo

Bunny Rescuer. Janet Walker at twelve. (Critter Alley)

Still Helping Wildlife. Janet Walker holds a young woodchuck, the only survivor when a bulldozer tore through her underground nest, killing her family. The woodchuck suffered a broken leg, which was set in a tiny cast. She recovered completely and was released. (Critter Alley)

games. Children from all over Michigan participated in "Walk for Wildlife," the center's annual fund-raiser.

During the winter, Walker traveled around the state and presented "Speaking of Wildlife," a program about Michigan's wild backyard neighbors. She advised people on what to do if they find animals that need help, and she encouraged them to learn about wild animals.

"If I knew each one of you individually, I would appreciate you a lot better than just knowing you as a group," Walker told her audience. "It's the same with wildlife. Learn about each species and you will understand and appreciate all animals."

Young Volunteer. Fourteen-year-old Jennifer Sovey releases orphaned bunnies raised at the center. Jennifer was an important part of the Junior Volunteer Program. (Critter Alley)

Three's a Charm

A full moon shone on the red fox as she trotted along a hunting trail, a young kit behind her. Lifting her black nose to the sky, the mother fox sniffed the air: mice, across the road. Quickly she loped ahead, looking back once to make sure the kit was keeping up. Suddenly a monster roared down the road, blinding her with its two powerful beams of light.

The mother fox froze, then tried to leap across the road, but the car hit her, flinging her lifeless body onto the shoulder. A second later the young fox slammed down beside her. Whimpering, the kit tried to get up, but she could barely lift her head.

Walking for Wildlife. Left to right, Terry Kimball and her two children, Ashley and Dustin Bofysil (and Sebastian the dog), help raise funds for Critter Alley. (Critter Alley)

Another car whizzed by, but this one stopped and backed up. The young kit lifted her head again. Her heart thumped in panic—humans! She knew she should run away, as she had been taught. But the pain in her head and body drained all her energy. She lost consciousness. The kit never heard the people

Saved. *An orphaned fox kit. (Critter Alley)*

Good as New. *The rehabilitated young fox was released with her new family. (Critter Alley)*

whispering. She did not feel them tenderly pick up her broken body and carry it to the car. The people knew about Critter Alley, so they took the young fox there. Because of their quick action, the young fox was treated immediately for shock, and her life was saved. Later rehabbers discovered that the kit had a broken leg and pelvis as well as a head injury.

By the next day the fox kit's condition was stable, and she was taken to a veterinarian for repair of her broken leg and pelvis. She then returned to Critter Alley for recovery. The little fox improved slowly over the next few days. Several weeks later a young male fox about the same age was brought to the center. The two fox kits roomed together. They became fast friends, sleeping together with their bushy, white-tipped tails wrapped around them.

Then an adult female fox that had been raised at a nature center was admitted to Critter Alley. Rehabilitators planned to teach her how to be wild so she could be released. The kits barked with excitement when they saw the adult fox, and the vixen treated the bright-eyed, romping kits as if they were her own. Together they learned more ways of the wild. By the end of summer, the black-stockinged trio was ready for release. Rehabilitators set them free in a thick forest surrounded by a lake and open fields. It was paradise for a frisky family of foxes.

Leaping for Liberty

Caesar and Sweetie, two bobcats, were admitted to Critter Alley after their owner was evicted from his property. The owner had raised the bobcats for breeding so he could sell the babies. For years, Caesar and Sweetie had lived in tiny, filthy cages. Their only food was pig liver and heart mixed with water once a day. The owner, who was afraid of the bobcats, teased and abused them.

When the bobcats arrived at Critter Alley, Caesar was seven years old. Born in captivity, he had spent his life being moved from one cramped, muddy cage to another. Sweetie, who was five years old, had known the wild only briefly when she was young before she was captured and caged.

Critter Alley's goal was to rehabilitate the cats and return them to the wild. The first step was to build new living quarters for them, and soon each bobcat had a cage big enough to run around and climb in. Then the cats were started on a new diet of road-killed animals, the same type of food they would be eating in the wild.

It took almost two years to teach Caesar and Sweetie the skills they would need to survive in the wild. They had to learn everything from scratch—how to hunt, hide, chase prey, and stay

Bobcat Haven. *With a roomy and clean home, good food, and caring people, Sweetie was learning how to be a wild bobcat again. (Critter Alley)*

Heading for the Hills. *After two years of rehabilitation at Critter Alley, Caesar was set free. (Critter Alley)*

away from humans. Finally it was time for release. Finding the perfect bobcat habitat had taken many months. Twelve volunteers escorted a snarling, spitting Caesar to the release site. A volunteer opened the cage door, and Caesar stepped out. He sniffed the air and looked around him in wonder. Then, not wasting a second, Caesar bolted for the wild, free at last!

Sadly, Sweetie never left Critter Alley. Because of the abuse she had suffered over the years, her poor health got worse. She died two months after Caesar sprang into freedom.

Opossum Release. (Critter Alley)

Apple a Day. *While recovering from a car-hit injury, a beaver enjoys a favorite treat.* (Critter Alley)

7

Rehabilitating Marine Animals

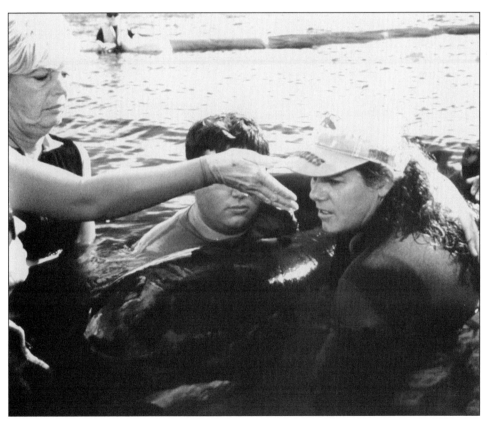

Dramatic Whale Rescue. *Volunteers from the Marine Mammal Conservancy and Wildlife Rescue of the Florida Keys help Tyson, a stranded pilot whale, stay afloat. Volunteers are (left to right) Rosemary Farrell, Eric Watson, and Chris Schulz. (Doug Franklin)*

If you have ever jumped into a cold pool or lake, you know how quickly water chills your body—a lot faster than air at the same temperature. Sea animals would chill, too, without thick layers of blubber or dense fur to protect them. Marine animals burn a lot of energy trying to stay warm. When they don't get enough food, they become weak, cold, and more likely to catch diseases. If pollution or violent storms add more stress to their bodies, survival becomes difficult, if not impossible.

Marine animals are admitted to rehabilitation centers because they are sick; injured; malnourished; or suffering from the effects of severe weather, pollution, or encounters with people. Also, young animals separated from their mothers need human help in order to survive.

Separated from Mom. An orphaned sea lion pup, not old enough to swim on his own, was rescued and taken to The Marine Mammal Center. (© 1997 The Marine Mammal Center/Photo: Ken Bach)

There are special challenges to rehabilitating marine animals. Most are big animals, needing enormous amounts of food and giant holding tanks. They also need highly skilled rehabilitators who know their natural history. Cetaceans (dolphins, whales, and porpoises) have strong family bonds. If rehabilitators want cooperation from family members, they need to understand and respect the animals' family ties. Another consideration is how marine animals breathe.

"Cetaceans are *conscious breathers*," explained Becky Barron, director of Wildlife Rescue of the Florida Keys. "That means they have to be awake in order to breathe. We humans breathe all the time, even when we're in a coma or under anesthesia."

Because of the problem of conscious breathing, surgery is almost out of the question for cetaceans, Barron said. The animals would stop breathing if they received anesthesia unless they were put on ventilators.

Problems out of Water

What if a dolphin or sea turtle needs an X-ray? No problem—unless electrical equipment is dropped accidentally into the tank of water. Because of the danger of electric shock to both humans and their patients, marine animals have to be removed from water before electrical equipment can be used. Such transfers are very stressful, especially for giant animals that have to be hoisted into the air and moved around by cranes. They can also be dangerous. In water cetaceans are buoyant, but when taken out of water, they can squash their own bodies with their massive weight. Sometimes marine mammals injure their internal organs or even suffocate themselves if they are kept out of water too long.

Freedom for Captive Animals?

If captive marine mammals—those taken from the wild to perform in marine parks and aquariums—are healthy, should they be rehabilitated and released back to the wild? For years many dolphins and orcas were taken by force from their families and used for entertainment and research purposes. No one worried about the effects on the captured animal and its family. Now we know a lot more about cetaceans, including the fact that their family structures are a lot like ours. When an orca or dolphin is taken away from its wild home, its family mourns, and the captive creature never stops yearning for its family.

Although there have been several successful releases of rehabilitated cetaceans, some authorities worry that captive animals will carry diseases to wild populations or that they will starve to death outside marine parks. Programs for successfully rehabilitating and releasing cetaceans must include some important steps, according to Rick Trout of Marine Mammal Conservancy (MMC) in Key Largo, Florida.

"The animals need to be healthy and relatively young," Trout said. "They should spend about a month in protected water near the release site, to get used to the sea. And they should be released in their home waters, where they were first captured."

If captive cougars and bobcats can learn to survive in the wild, why can't cetaceans, which are more intelligent? Should they be given the chance?

The Marine Mammal Center

Location: Marin Headlands
1065 Fort Cronkhite
Sausalito, CA 94965
415-289-7325
www.tmmc.org
E-mail: admin@tmmc.org

Description: Large center treating more than 600 marine mammals a year, many of which are endangered or threatened species

Staff: 45 paid positions, including veterinarians, biologists, veterinary technicians, and educators; 800 volunteers

Funding: Memberships, donations, fund-raisers, gift shop

Newsletter: *Release*

Programs: Many—at the center and off-site

Tours: Yes, at the center and at Pier 39 Interpretive Center; 1 gift shop at each location

Making a Splash. The Marine Mammal Center volunteers help an elephant seal pup into a pool. (© 1997 The Marine Mammal Center/ Photo: Ken Bach)

The Marine Mammal Center (TMMC) was started in the 1970s as a tiny operation run by volunteers who transported sick and injured animals in the backseats of their cars and fed the animals at night by the light of car headlights.

Today TMMC is the largest marine mammal rehabilitation center in the country. Located on seven acres of land, the center is made up of a veterinary hospital with animal pens and pools, an intensive care unit, laboratories, and offices. Veterinarians, veterinary technicians, biologists, educators, and volunteers work there. In addition to the main hospital staff, TMMC has rescue teams stationed along the California coast. Volunteers care for sick or injured animals at two holding places until they can be transferred to the main center.

Every year hundreds of marine animals—seals, sea lions, whales, dolphins, and sea otters—are rehabilitated at TMMC. More than eight hundred volunteers assist in all areas of rehabilitation. Members (thirty-five thousand) and donors provide most of the financial support.

Van Gogh. *Notice the scars? This California sea lion was caught in a fishing net that became wound too tightly around his head and neck. Like his famous namesake, van Gogh lost an ear (flap). (© 1997 The Marine Mammal Center/ Photo: Jane Oka)*

Research

In addition to rescue and rehabilitation, TMMC conducts important research. Scientists study marine mammal diseases, animal behavior and nutrition, and the effects of pollution and severe weather on ocean mammals. The center also participates in California's oil response program. Staff and volunteers are active in helping to protect critical coastal habitat.

Hands-on Education

One of the many education programs offered by TMMC involves learning about the natural history of sea lions while watching hundreds of wild sea lions climb onto the floating docks at Pier 39 in San Francisco's Fisherman's Wharf. Instructors also teach classes at the center and visit schools and communities, sometimes traveling in TMMC's Sea Van, the "classroom on wheels."

TMMC educators inform people about the marine world and how to protect it. All education programs are available in Spanish. The center also offers guided coastal outings, which include taking beach walks, exploring tide pools, and watching whales from the shore.

Helping Humphrey

People couldn't believe their eyes when they spotted a humpback whale in San Francisco Bay in 1985. Gliding under the Golden Gate Bridge, the whale (named Humphrey) swam through two more bays and under three more bridges. For the next three weeks, Humphrey cruised up the Sacramento

River in fresh water that became increasingly shallow. Everyone who saw him worried that the giant would beach because, weighing in at forty tons, Humphrey was definitely too big for a river!

The Marine Mammal Center rescue team worked with hundreds of other volunteers to save Humphrey. At first rescuers banged on pipes, making loud noises underwater to drive the whale back toward the bay. Once he was in the bay, rescuers played recordings of humpback whales feeding. The sound was music to Humphrey! He followed the boat across the bay, under the Golden Gate Bridge, and into the Pacific Ocean. The wayward whale was saved.

In 1990 Humphrey swam into San Francisco Bay again, heading inland. This time he got stuck in the mud. TMMC's rescue team and medical experts worked frantically to free Humphrey. After three exhausting days and nights, they freed him, and the huge whale glided back into the Pacific Ocean.

Stuck in the Mud. *Three TMMC staff members evaluate Humphrey's condition while the unfortunate humpback whale is beached. They are (left to right) Jan Roletto, curator; Ken Lee, stranding coordinator; and Laurie Gage, veterinarian. (© 1997 The Marine Mammal Center/Photo: Ken Bach)*

No one knows what has happened to the wandering whale since then. Many people expected a repeat performance in 1995, since Humphrey's first two visits had occurred five years apart. In the spring of that year, a whale that looked like Humphrey was spotted in Baja, California, but it wisely stayed away from San Francisco Bay.

An Otterly Bad Hair Day

Jambo, an endangered California sea otter, was not doing well on his own. Recently weaned, the young otter was cold and thin, and his fur was matted. He was rescued and taken to TMMC.

Otters are the only marine animals without blubber. Instead, they have two layers of dense fur. Otter fur—with about one million hairs per square inch—is the thickest of all mammal fur. (Human hair is only about one-eighth as dense as otter fur.) When an otter rolls in the water, air becomes trapped between the two layers of fur and acts like a wetsuit, holding in the otter's body heat. Otters need to groom themselves constantly to keep their fur free of food and dirt. If the fur becomes matted, it cannot fluff up and trap air, and it loses its ability to repel water.

Jambo was kept in a tote (portable pen) with a pool of water that could be covered to keep him out. Because his fur was in such miserable shape, he chilled quickly, so Jambo was allowed only quick dips in the cool water. (Warm water cannot be used with otters because it damages their fur.) Each time Jambo came out of the water, rehabilitators had to dry him off and warm him under a lamp. In the wild, otters burn many calories staying warm. To fuel all that energy, they eat constantly, just as Jambo had to do. Exhausted rehabilitators had to let Jambo into his pool to eat every few hours around the clock because otters usually eat floating on their backs in the water. Using their chests as tables, they hammer clams, mussels, and other shellfish with rocks.

Seafood Snacks. Jambo, an endangered California sea otter, eats in his pool at TMMC. (© 1997 The Marine Mammal Center/Photo: Ken Bach)

Each time Jambo finished a seafood meal, the staff supervised his grooming, making sure his fur was thoroughly cleaned, because without good grooming habits, Jambo would not survive in the wild. With all the skilled attention he got, Jambo improved quickly. In preparation for release, he was moved to a large pool and given live food. A few weeks later Jambo was released to his Morro Bay home, where he now lives an otterly well-groomed life.

David A. Straz, Jr., Manatee Hospital

Location: Lowry Park Zoo
1101 W. Sligh Avenue
Tampa, FL 33604
813-935-8552
www.lowryparkzoo.org
E-mail: information@lowryparkzoo.org

Description: The only nonprofit hospital in the world dedicated to rehabilitating sick, injured, and orphaned manatees

Staff: Zoo staff and volunteers

Funding: Lowry Park Zoo budget, private donations

Newsletter: Yes, with zoo membership

Programs: Educational exhibits with live manatees, kids' sleepovers

Tours: Yes, as part of Lowry Park Zoo admission

Manatee Emergency Room. *Lowry Park Zoo's animal care staff receives a manatee suffering from the effects of red tide. (Dale Moore)*

In 1972 the West Indian manatee was placed on the Endangered Species List. Today, there are only about three thousand manatees left in the United States. The David A. Straz, Jr., Manatee Hospital is an important place because it provides rehabilitation for individual animals, research studies to learn more about protecting the species, and vital education for the public.

Mystery Disease

During the spring of 1996 more than 150 manatees died from a mysterious illness. State and federal scientists worked frantically to identify the cause. As the only center treating sick, live animals, the manatee hospital cared for thirteen to fifteen manatees at once. Zoo vets began to notice dramatic improvements in many of the animals after they had been given around-the-clock care and kept in clean water for a few days. These observations helped identify the cause of the manatee die-off—red tide.

Red tide is discolored seawater caused by blooming algae. In large concentrations, red tide is toxic to marine animals because it affects their nervous systems and causes muscle spasms and paralysis. Animals may drown if not rescued.

Because manatees reproduce slowly, they will not survive as a species if too many animals die off at once. Natural disasters, as well as human activities, keep manatees in constant danger of extinction. The gentle sea cows spend much of their time in shallow water, feeding on sea grass and other plants. They have to surface to breathe, and that is when they are often hit by speeding boats. Nearly all adults have slash scars from boat propellers. Loud boats also disrupt the animals' mating rituals and social gatherings.

Protecting and Supporting Manatees

Florida has taken steps to help its official state mammal. There are now twenty-two "protection zones" in places where manatees normally gather. Boats must go slowly through these zones from November 15 to March 31.

Habitat destruction, waterway gates, pollution, and cold weather also injure and kill manatees. Because they cannot survive for long in water cooler than 68 degrees, manatees spend winters in Florida, usually in warm natural springs or by hydroelectric plants. Sometimes, though, even Florida is hit with chilly winters, which means trouble for manatees. Some, especially the younger ones, develop life-threatening hypothermia. The David A. Straz, Jr., Manatee Hospital has rehabilitated more than one hundred manatees since it opened in 1991. It has X-ray and ultrasound equipment, an operating room, veterinary offices, and three large rehabilitation pools. The hospital is located behind the scenes of the Manatee and Aquatic Center at Lowry Park Zoo, where more than half a million people visit the manatee exhibit every year. While the visitors

Scarred for Life. Most manatees have slash scars from speedboat propellers. (Shannon K. Jacobs)

Special Manatee Pools. *Lowry Park Zoo's David A. Straz, Jr., Manatee Hospital has a series of interconnecting pools. Up to sixteen manatees can be held and treated at one time. Shift gates allow zoo vets to move animals from pool to pool or to quarantine them, if needed. (Richard Wilhelm)*

watch live sea cows forage for carrots and lettuce from underwater viewing tanks, they learn how to protect these endangered animals and their habitat.

Taking care of manatees is expensive. Half of the zoo's annual animal department budget is spent on manatee rehabilitation. Food for just one manatee costs $27,000 a year. To keep properly filtered water in the tanks at 74 degrees, the hospital uses 100 gallons of propane and $160 worth of electricity every day.

How can people help the David A. Straz, Jr., Manatee Hospital?

"Visit the zoo and learn all you can about manatees," suggested Sam Winslow, Lowry Park's director of collections. "People also can adopt a manatee for $35 or more. If you can't contribute money, you can always volunteer at the zoo."

Volunteer divers help by vacuuming the manatee tanks every morning, which saves the paid staff at least two hours a day.

Manatee hospital staff and Amber Wildlife, a volunteer group, transport recovered manatees to release sites. Manatees are so popular in Florida that often several hundred people line up along the riverbanks to welcome the sea cows home.

Starting Anew

Newbob, an orphaned baby manatee, got his name from the man who found him (Bob) and the day he was rescued (New Year's Day). Newbob's mother had been crushed and killed in a lock in Lake Okeechobee. When admitted, Newbob weighed only 129 pounds, and he would not eat. He was sent to Homosassa Springs, a wildlife park and sanctuary for manatees, because the staff hoped that one of two nursing females at the springs would become Newbob's foster mother. But that didn't happen, and Newbob was returned to the hospital.

The following spring Newbob went to Merritt Island, a 240-acre National Wildlife Refuge on Florida's east coast that serves as a halfway house for manatees. There they learn how to forage for their natural foods in the seawater. Once again Newbob's fickle appetite let him down, so back to the hospital he went. The staff there gave him lots of lettuce, carrots, and high-protein biscuits, fattening him up to 1,100 pounds.

Lucky Frank

For a while Newbob shared a pool with Lucky Frank, a juvenile manatee that was admitted with hypothermia. Weak and

Manatee Sanctuary. Manatees are fed well at Homosassa Springs. (Shannon K. Jacobs)

underweight when rescued, Lucky Frank had developed several infections. After successfully treating the infections, the hospital staff focused on Lucky Frank's poor eating habits. They put the two young manatees together, hoping Newbob would influence Lucky Frank. It worked! Inspired by his older friend, Lucky Frank became a hearty consumer of lettuce, and his weight increased. Meanwhile, Newbob continued to improve. Both manatees recov-

ered so well that they were released together. The zoo staff was hoping the two sea-cow pals would stay together, but Lucky Frank headed upstream on his own. Newbob was fitted with a satellite-tracking belt so his progress could be followed.

Dr. David Murphy, Lowry Park Zoo veterinarian, caught up with Newbob in the wild and drew a blood sample. Lab results showed just what the hospital staff was hoping—that Newbob was healthy and doing well in his wild home.

Great Success Story. Lucky Frank works on his appetite while healing from cold-water stress. He arrived at Manatee Hospital in February 1996 and was released a year later, in the spring. (Richard Wilhelm)

Texas State Aquarium

Location: 2710 N. Shoreline Boulevard
Corpus Christi, TX 78402
361-881-1200 or 800-477-GULF
www.texasstateaquarium.org
E-mail: mermaid@txstateaq.org

Description: Large 7.3-acre center on the beach, with exhibits and re-created habitats; 150 animals treated a year

Staff: 80 paid staff, 300 volunteers

Funding: Memberships, admission fees, programs, donations

Newsletter: *Star,* members' quarterly newsletter

Programs: Daily and educational; on- and off-site

Tours: Available

The Gladys Sue Albertson Memorial Rehabilitation Program at the Texas State Aquarium (TSA) is the only program on the Texas coast dedicated to treating birds, sea turtles, and marine mammals. Nonreleasable animals are used in daily programs to educate people about the dangers the animals face and how people can help them.

TSA has exciting exhibits showing sea life in the Gulf of Mexico. One of them, "Turtle Bend," is an artificial turtle habitat that serves as a home for sick, orphaned, and injured sea turtles. Six turtles (including an endangered Kemp's ridley) live inside the exhibit tank, and several others are being treated behind the scenes. Two of the rehabilitating turtles are olive ridley hatchlings, which are cousins to Kemp's ridleys. They were brought to TSA after hatching at the Dallas Zoo. The eggs had been confiscated from a woman who tried to sneak them illegally into the United States from Central America. When the sea turtle babies are big enough to survive on their own, they will be released in waters off Costa Rica.

Turtle Bend. *Young visitors watch sea turtles during the 1995 grand opening of Texas State Aquarium's re-created turtle habitat. (Helen Swetman)*

A juvenile Kemp's ridley sea turtle named Snapper was hit by a speedboat off the coast of New York. Because of permanent injuries, the sea turtle cannot survive in the wild, so the aquarium is his permanent home.

Sea Turtle Research

One of the aquarium's research projects involves tracking sea turtles. The project aims to teach students about sea turtles as well as to increase the population of Kemp's ridleys.

Teachers and students from area high schools help collect information on several Kemp's ridleys, which are fitted with satellite transmitters. The teachers and students have traveled to the ridleys' only known remaining nesting place in Mexico, where they helped protect eggs, release hatchlings, and tag more turtles for the next study.

School and community groups are welcome to tour the aquarium's 7.3 acres. TSA educators visit schools, using slide shows, theater productions, and hands-on marine displays to teach about life in the sea and how humans affect it. A mobile exhibit, "Ocean in Motion," takes the Gulf of Mexico to thousands of schools around the state. The aquarium also hosts SeaCamp, a marine science day camp for kids aged six to fifteen, and a live satellite show called "Wonders Under the Sea."

Sea Turtle. A Kemp's ridley turtle. (Helen Swetman)

Stranded in the Lone Star State

More than 120 dolphins washed ashore along the Texas coast in 1994. Most of them died, but a few live animals were treated at the Texas State Aquarium. Volunteers from TSA and the Texas Marine Mammal Stranding Network (part of a national volunteer group) stayed with the dolphins day and night. They swam the animals around in holding tanks, trying to keep their blowholes above water so the dolphins would not drown.

One young male Atlantic bottlenose dolphin named Double Trouble suffered from a respiratory infection, like the other dolphins. But he improved quickly and began swimming on his own. Soon Double Trouble was strong enough to be a candidate for release—a very rare situation for a stranded marine animal. An animal is considered stranded when it goes into shallow water or other water where it normally would not go and seems to be in distress. Usually animals are so sick or injured by the time they strand that they do not recover.

Double Trouble was tagged with a satellite-tracking device that allowed researchers to follow his movements in the wild. Then he was loaded by stretcher into a box especially designed for him. Volunteers moved Double Trouble onto a truck and ferried him across a channel, then lifted the box by crane onto a research boat. The boat motored ten miles offshore, where the crane lowered Double Trouble into the water. He was released.

Double Trouble set a record that day. He was the first dolphin in Texas history to survive a stranding, go through rehabilitation, and be released. At that time, only four such dolphin rehabilitations and releases had taken place in the United States.

Few marine mammals survive strandings, even with excellent rehabilitation care. They would be better protected if we all worked to prevent pollution, which may be responsible for making some animals sick and causing them to strand.

Double Trouble. A Texas Marine Mammal Stranding Network volunteer feeds Double Trouble during the dolphin's stay at TSA's rehabilitation and education facility, Sea Lab. (Helen Swetman)

Wildlife Rescue of the Florida Keys

Location: 1801 White Street
Key West, FL 33040
305-294-1441
www.keywestwildlife.com/rescue.htm
E-mail: WildlifeRescueKw@aol.com

Description: Medium-sized center treating native Florida wildlife, including marine animals

Staff: Director and volunteers

Funding: Memberships, donations, fund-raisers

Newsletter: Yes

Programs: Yes, at the center, for young people and some adults

Tours: By request

Like many rehabilitators, Becky Barron began her wildlife work as a veterinary technician. As director of Wildlife Rescue of the Florida Keys, she assists with dolphin and whale rescues. She also supervises the rehabilitation of more than a thousand land mammals, birds, and reptiles every year.

Wildlife Rescue offers several practical educational programs for children. One of them, "Kids and Critters Club," is for seven- to eleven-year-olds. The weekly program mixes environmental activities with hands-on care of animals. Children help prepare the animals' food, feed a few of the calm critters, and help with bandages.

Piloting the Whales

Barron was among three thousand volunteers who helped rescue four pilot whales that stranded near her home in

Fish Food. *Becky Barron cuts up fish to feed gulls, pelicans, and other birds at the wildlife center. (Shannon K. Jacobs)*

Elvis. *Volunteers hold Elvis firmly while other whales are being treated. (Chris Schulz)*

Big Pine Key in 1995. The whales were too sick to swim. Volunteers worked in four-hour shifts, holding them up to keep them from sinking and drowning.

The adult female whale was named Kandi, after the young woman who pulled her from the sea bottom. Kandi's juvenile son was called Tyson (after the boxer Mike Tyson) because of all his scars. The other two males were a frisky juvenile orphan dubbed Dennis (as in Dennis the Menace) and Elvis, who probably was Kandi's mate.

This was the first time in U.S. history that whales were rehabilitated by volunteers in open water, according to Rick Trout, director of husbandry at Marine Mammal Conservancy in Key Largo. Volunteers from MMC and Wildlife Rescue of the Florida Keys joined together to coordi-

Floating the Whales. *Volunteers near Key West hold up a stranded pilot whale to keep it from drowning. (Doug Franklin)*

nate the rescue, rehabilitation, and release of the whales. One of the major challenges of working with the whales in open water was ensuring that every person knew what to do. Nearly one hundred volunteers a day had to be trained quickly. Trout and Barron supervised volunteers, tube-fed and medicated the whales, and regularly drew blood to check the health of the animals.

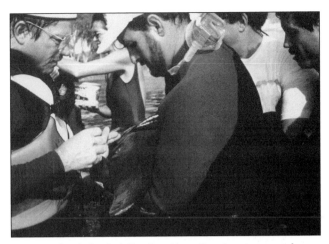

A Way with Whales. *Rick Trout's understanding of marine mammals helped create a safe experience for all. Trout (left) and Robert Lingenfelser (middle), MMC president, draw blood from a whale. To their right is volunteer John Powers. (Doug Franklin)*

"The most life-threatening situation was dehydration," explained Lynne Stringer, MMC animal care technician. "The animals were exposed to sun, and they were not eating fish, which is where they usually get their fluids."

The whales were tube-fed blenderized "fish shakes" three times a day. After gently prying open a whale's mouth, Barron and Stringer inserted a garden-hose-sized tube into the first stomach compartment (whales have three stomach compartments). Then they poured in the fish gruel. Not surprisingly, the whales disliked the intubations. Even sick pilot whales could easily injure or kill people, yet these animals hurt no one. Why were they so cooperative? Barron gave most of the credit to Trout, who is a former dolphin trainer.

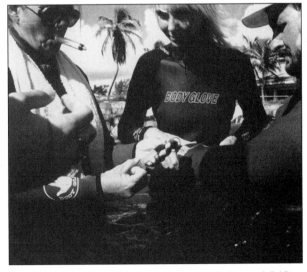

Blood Tests. *From left to right, Becky Barron; Lynne Stringer, MMC animal care technician; and Robert Lingenfelser, MMC president, draw blood from a whale. (Doug Franklin)*

"We spent half the time nursing these animals and half the time learning what was acceptable behavior in dealing with different family members," she said. "Rick taught the rest of us to be constantly aware of things, such as a whale giving a little tap with a pectoral fin or moving its body in a certain way, warning you not to do something."

When the whales became stronger, they were moved to a nearby, unused boat basin with deeper water. Volunteers wore float jackets to stay up. They kept the whales afloat by holding strips of foam under them like water wings. Volunteers sprayed the whales with ice water to keep them from overheating. They also gave the animals physical therapy, swimming them and massaging their muscles.

The community of Big Pine Key generously pitched in. Some people volunteered as whale rescuers. Others provided supplies, food, tents, and portable toilets for the thousands of helpers. Luckily, the whales had stranded near a resort. Owners of the Mariner Resort let exhausted volunteers take showers and nap in vacant rooms.

The whales were eating better by the second week. Then tragedy struck. Dennis, the 450-pound juvenile, dove too deeply one day while playing in a canal and got stuck in the mud. Before he could be rescued, Dennis inhaled some of the mud. He soon died of pneumonia. A week later Elvis developed complications from a lung infection and died. The deaths were hard for the surviving whales as well as for the humans. Kandi and Tyson lost their appetites and energy. But they slowly began to improve as volunteers showered them with encouragement and attention.

Finally, after two months of treatment, Kandi and Tyson were ready for release. First they were tagged and freeze-branded (a painless tattoo used for identification). Then the whales were loaded onto a seventy-four-foot U.S. Navy landing craft. Special cushioned stretchers held up the seven-hundred-pound Tyson and his one-thousand-pound mother. The ship took the marine mammals and forty volunteers fifteen miles out to sea, where the whales were released. Three days later Kandi

Delicate Cargo. *A U.S. Navy landing craft prepares to load volunteers and whales. (Chris Schulz)*

and Tyson were spotted from the air. They were swimming and feeding with a pod of dolphins.

Strandings

Nobody knows exactly why whales strand. The animals could be sick, old, confused, or full of parasites. Pollution may also be a factor.

Going in Style. Tyson rests on a special waterbed aboard the ship. Volunteer Chris Schulz keeps him cool with towels soaked in ice water. In the next bed, Tyson's mother, Kandi, gets the same treatment. (Chris Schulz)

"Scientists are finding toxins in the body tissues of a lot of dead marine mammals," Barron said. "We find toxins in many animals we work with."

One of Trout's theories is that stranding is a protection against drowning. "Whales are as frightened of drowning as humans are," he explained. "That's why they go to beaches when they get sick instead of heading into deep waters."

Whatever the reason, Trout and Barron agreed that stranded animals should not be pushed offshore. "Whales strand for a reason," Barron said. "Rarely do they make a wrong turn and come fifteen miles into shore. They probably need treatment."

"If you see a stranded whale, call the Coast Guard or Marine Patrol right away," Barron suggested. "They will contact qualified people to check the animals. They also will explain what you can do until the experts arrive."

If you want to do some online research to prepare for encountering stranded

Rescued, Rehabilitated, and Released. Kandi and Tyson were saved because of thousands of brave, skillful, and dedicated people who assisted in their recovery. (Doug Franklin)

or injured marine animals, do an Internet search for "Marine Mammal Health and Stranding Response Program." This site describes the National Marine Fisheries Service program for collecting information about and coordinating effective responses to marine mammal strandings. It also lists names, addresses, and phone numbers of NMFS regional stranding coordinators for the six regions into which the United States is divided. To find out which region your state is in, click on "Map of Marine Mammal Stranding Networks" on the home page of this site to see a color-coded map of the United States.

8

Rehabilitating Birds

Screechers. *Three juvenile screech owls, each with different personalities, were rehabilitated at Wild Care, Inc., on Cape Cod. (Karen Von den Deale)*

Just as some mammals fatten up for hibernation, many birds eat like crazy too. But they don't hibernate. They migrate.

Migration

Over 80 percent of birds that breed in North America migrate. In the fall birds travel thousands of miles, often to Central and South America, where the weather is warm and food is abundant. In the spring many birds wing northward to Canada and Alaska to nest and raise their young.

On any spring or autumn night, millions of birds fly over the United States. Scientists have calculated the numbers by watching through telescopes focused on the moon and counting birds flying past. Some birds travel at night and some in the daytime; a few do both. Although each species has its own route, birds generally follow four U.S. migration flyways: the Atlantic, Mississippi, Central (Great Plains and Rocky Mountains), and Pacific.

Migration is filled with dangers every wingbeat of the way. Because birds cross state and country lines, they may go from being protected in one area to being hunted in another. They often face storms, headwinds that sap their energy, and predators that capture or kill them.

Risky Rest Stops

While a few birds travel nonstop to their destinations, many

Poisoned. Like many hungry migrating raptors, this eagle ate a dead animal. But the carcass had been poisoned to kill predators such as coyotes. (Michael Judish)

rest in stopover places, which is why people in Connecticut might see tropical birds migrating from South America. These rest stops are very important for migrating birds, but they also can be risky. Tired and hungry birds sometimes discover that the trees they rested in the year before are gone, replaced by homes or shops. Their water sources may have dried up. In some places birds are shot out of the sky for target practice, attacked by cats, or poisoned. Birds also get trapped in six-pack ring holders or fishing line while swimming or bathing in water. A few migrating water birds have landed on what they thought was water only to discover, too late, that it was a shiny, wet parking lot.

Habitat Loss Tragedy

Habitats at both ends of migration routes are shrinking as people cut down forests and drain wetlands. When waterways shrink, more water birds are forced to share space, which makes the threat of disease more serious. One sick duck can infect a lake full of waterfowl.

Recently scientists have documented a decline in the numbers of some songbirds and other migrating birds. This population reduction may be attributable to hazards the birds face during migration as well as their shrinking habitats. If birds have not put on enough fat before migration, they lose strength and can't keep up with their flock. The young, sick, and injured sometimes cannot keep up either. These are the birds that often end up with rehabilitators.

Rehabilitators work with many kinds of birds, and some specialize in certain species such as raptors, water birds, or even tiny, jeweled hummingbirds.

Hummingbird Feeding. (Urban Wildlife Rescue)

Alaska Raptor Center

Location: 1000 Raptor Way
PO Box 2984
Sitka, AK 99835
907-747-8662
www.alaskaraptor.org
E-mail: programs.alaskaraptor@alaska.com

Description: Large center treating about 200 raptors and other birds a year

Staff: 18 full-time-equivalent paid staff members, including a full-time staff avian vet and several bird handlers; 65 volunteers from all over the world who donate 3,500-plus hours annually

Funding: Donations, memberships, bird adoptions, classes, grants, gift-shop sales

Newsletter: *The Mew Review,* published quarterly

Programs: At the center, in schools, and around the country

Tours: Open for summer tours 8–4 p.m. Monday through Friday and at other times when cruise ships visit Sitka in the summer

Like many wildlife rehabilitation centers, Alaska Raptor Center began in someone's backyard. Two men dedicated to healing an injured bald eagle and protecting raptors in Alaska started the center in 1980. From those humble beginnings, Alaska Raptor Center has grown into a seventeen-acre avian care facility known throughout the world. About two hundred eagles, hawks, owls, falcons, and other species of birds are rehabilitated there annually.

The center's three-pronged mission—rehabilitation, education, and research—is being fulfilled with an important new addition: a twenty-thousand-square-foot, state-of-the-art bald eagle flight-training facility. The facility was badly needed because an unusually heavy snowfall crushed the center's flight barn a few years ago. Large birds such as eagles need a lot of room to exercise their wings and build up their flight muscles. However, with no suitable space, Alaska Raptor Cen-

Hoot. *A barred owl at the Sitka, Alaska, Raptor Rehabilitation Center. (Farmer)*

ter's eagles had to be taken to Montana for flight conditioning. The long trips were grueling for the birds and their handlers. Over the course of a few years, and with the enthusiastic help of the center's forty thousand annual visitors and members, $2.5 million was raised to construct a new facility.

"With the completion of our new facility, Alaska Raptor Center is now among the leading avian care facilities in the world," said Executive Director Elizabeth Whealy.

Education

A key component of Alaska Raptor Center's educational experience is that it allows visitors to be close to live birds. In the past, visitors observed and learned from the twenty-five or so nonreleasable raptors who live at the center, but they were not allowed near birds being rehabilitated. The new flight facility has changed that because the center has installed specially designed one-way glass to separate the public from the recuperating raptors. Visitors can watch the birds' fascinating wild behavior and learn about their natural history, but the birds never see or hear the visitors.

"Now you can watch a recovering eagle twelve feet away as it fishes for salmon in a waterfall in our coastal rainforest exhibit," Whealy said. "Or visitors can hear eagles as they glide around obstacles in the flight tubes."

Rehabilitation

Diagnosing sick or injured animals can be difficult sometimes because birds—especially eagles—are experts at hiding injuries or weaknesses. The flight-training facility enables the center's medical staff to observe their eagle patients closely in a natural setting. The staff can also set up flying obstacles for birds who need to increase their strength and agility. This approach speeds up diagnosis and treatment and decreases the amount of time the eagles have to spend in captivity.

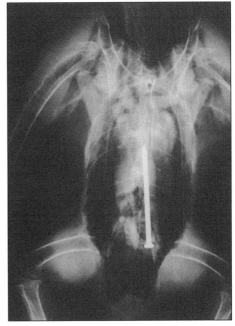

Spiked. An X-ray of a sick eagle showed a 3 3/4" nail he'd ingested. Spike was released 48 hours later, after emergency surgery saved his life. (Alaska Raptor Center)

In addition to returning hundreds of healthy bald eagles to the wild, Alaska Raptor Center sends nonreleasable eagles to the lower forty-eight states for breeding programs. The offspring of these birds are set free.

Research

The flight-training facility gives researchers many opportunities to observe the behavior of birds of prey in as natural a setting as possible. Data gathered from these observations enhance treatment methods for injured birds and enlarge the body of knowledge about raptors in general.

Programs for Schools and Families

Visitors to Alaska Raptor Center have some choices: they can experience raptors up close when they tour the center, where they are encouraged to ask questions about the majestic birds; they can visit the raptors in residence in outdoor enclosures that were built into the natural rainforest of Sitka; and they can walk around the nature trail that winds around the center and goes through four natural biozones. From the trail they are able to see old- and new-growth trees, native plants, and animals (including salmon) that live in the rainforest in abundance.

Passport to Raptors is a popular program for students on field trips or summer tours. Using the passport as a guide, children visit twelve education stations and learn about all types of raptors. They touch feathers and walk through the temperate rainforest to learn about native plants. They also meet the center's twenty-five raptors in residence. When students finish the whole series, a staff member takes their passport photos as they pose with a raptor.

One of Alaska Raptor Center's chief ambassadors, Volta, is a bald eagle that travels all over the country with his handler, visiting schools as part of the Alaska Air Warriors educational program. Volta's story is similar to that of many injured birds at the center: he was electrocuted when he flew into a power line. The fall caused a concussion and broke a shoulder bone that is critical for flight. Since he was not able

Volta. *Alaska Raptor Center's "chief ambassador."* (Thomas Cooper)

to fly again, Volta could not be released back to the wild, so he became an education bird. Volta helps children learn about Alaska, its magnificent birds, and the important part they play in our environment.

Any classroom in the world can adopt a raptor in residence. The donation helps the center pay for the bird's daily care and medical needs. This program is called Adopt-a-Raptor. Teachers receive ready-to-teach materials, including a ninety-page curriculum, to plan lessons and activities about raptors and their habitats. The class also receives a videotape, an adoption certificate, a photo of the adopted bird, and a one-year membership to Alaska Raptor Center.

The Teaching Eagle

One of Alaska Raptor Center's most popular and beloved birds was a bald eagle named Buddy. A nonreleasable education bird, Buddy traveled around the country with staff members, visiting schools and communities. Buddy could not be released because he had been human-imprinted when he was an eaglet and either fell from his nest or was stolen. The people who raised Buddy did not know much about baby raptors because they let the young eagle imprint on them. Then they abandoned him in an Alaskan village. Maybe they didn't know how helpless he was, or maybe they believed he would do what eagles do "naturally"—hunt. However, birds are not born knowing how to hunt and fish; they have to learn those skills from their parents.

After he was abandoned, Buddy walked around the village for weeks, begging for food. He was starving because he was used to being fed by people. In fact, Buddy thought he *was* people. One day, Buddy tried to snatch a red ball away from a child. He may have thought the ball was food, or he may have been trying to hunt or play. Although Buddy didn't hurt anyone, he scared the boy and his parents, who knew what razor-sharp talons could do to a child. The parents called the police and reported a dangerous eagle attacking a child. Buddy, the criminal eagle, was picked up

Buddy at School. *Buddy made friends all over the country when he visited schools and communities. (Kari Gabriel)*

and taken to Alaska Raptor Center, where rehabilitators fed him good eagle food and cared for him. One thing they could not fix, though, was his most serious injury—imprinting.

As Buddy matured into adulthood, his dark head and tail feathers turned white and his behavior began to change. He began building nests with sticks and grass and defending the nests, as mature eagles do in the wild. When he chose a human rehabilitator as a mate, it was clear how serious the human imprinting was.

In 1995, while on a tour in Los Angeles, Buddy died of a sudden illness. The beautiful eagle had made many friends in his short life. Buddy's magnificent presence reminded people everywhere that all wild creatures deserve to be healthy and free.

Maturing Buddy. As Buddy got older, his dark head and tail feathers turned white. (Amy Sweeney)

A Whale of a Spill

Bonnie and Clyde, two hungry young bald eagles, climbed inside a dead whale to feast on the meat. They didn't think about the oil greasing up their feathers. After they had filled their bellies, the eagles prepared for flight only to discover that they were grounded.

Twenty other eagles that had also been feeding on the whales died before they could be rescued. Because their feathers were oiled, the birds couldn't fly or stay warm. The dead eagles were found near the whale carcass. Bonnie and Clyde were luckier, and both eagles were taken to Alaska Raptor Center for rehabilitation. Clyde recovered quickly in two months, but Bonnie had trouble flying. Finally, after going through a vertical exercise program, Bonnie progressed well enough to be released to Alaska skies.

In a few years Bonnie will choose a mate. If she stays away from dead whales, traps, guns, small planes, and power lines, she will be able to enjoy a wild life for many years.

Bonnie. *The young bald eagle had trouble flying at first, during rehabilitation. (Harvey and Pamela Hergett)*

Clyde. *Recovering quickly, Clyde was released before Bonnie. (Harvey and Pamela Hergett)*

Suncoast Seabird Sanctuary

Location: 18328 Gulf Boulevard
Indian Shores, FL 33785
727-391-6211
www.seabirdsanctuary.org
E-mail: seabird@seabirdsanctuary.org

Description: Large wild bird rehabilitation center treating more than 7,000 birds a year; most are water birds

Staff: 20 full-time staff, 3 volunteer vets, many volunteers

Funding: Donations, memberships, fund-raisers, and corporate sponsors

Newsletter: *Suncoast Seabird Sanctuary,* published quarterly

Programs: Guided tours of center, monthly education programs

Tours: Yes; open 7 days a week, 9 a.m. to dark; free admission

A Friend of Birds. *Ralph Heath holds a disabled brown pelican that lives at Suncoast Seabird Sanctuary. The bird is blind in one eye. (Shannon K. Jacobs)*

Stopping to help a cormorant with a broken wing changed Ralph Heath's life in 1971 and also made the world a better place for hurt birds. Heath took the bird to a veterinarian, who pinned the broken wing. Naming the bird Maynard, Heath took him home to recover.

Cormorants eat a lot of fish. Luckily, local bait-shop owners generously donated food for Maynard. When word got out about Heath's healing touch, people began bringing him injured birds. Sometimes up to eighty birds a day were dropped off at his home clinic.

Being around injured animals was not new to Heath. Years before, he and other kids had taken hurt creatures to Heath's father, an orthopedic surgeon.

"My father's office was in Tampa," Heath explained. "When kids brought him injured animals, he'd keep them in boxes and operate on them if they needed it. I'd come home from school and watch him operate on the animals—squirrels, rabbits, turtles, and birds."

In 1972 Heath turned his beach home into the Suncoast Seabird Sanctuary. Since then it has grown into the largest wild bird hospital in the United States. A team of wildlife biologists, veterinary technicians, and volunteers rehabilitates and releases about seven thousand birds a year.

Suncoast Seabird Sanctuary is located on beachfront land on the Gulf of Mexico, where visitors can stroll around the sunny 1.5 acres. Thirty large aviaries are homes for birds that are permanent residents as well as those being prepared for release. In 2002 a new 2,500-square-foot avian hospital was completed. The floor plan of the $600,000 facility was designed by

Birds of Prey. *Raptors, such as these barn owls, come to the sanctuary from all over Florida. (Stan Ashbrook)*

Barbara Soto, an experienced hospital supervisor at the sanctuary.

Every day twenty to twenty-four birds arrive at the sanctuary. As many as six hundred birds may live and recover there at any given time. They eat more than five hundred pounds of fish, fruits, nuts, and meat a day. The annual cost of fish alone is $75,000.

Disabled Birds Thrive

Although Maynard the cormorant lived, he was not able to fly again. Heath got the proper permits so he could give the bird a home for the rest of his life. Many other disabled birds live at the sanctuary now with others of their species. Some have reproduced in captivity, and others have gone to zoos for captive breeding programs. By offering a home for permanently disabled birds that reproduce, the sanctuary has added

Rehabilitation Compound. *Recovering brown pelicans are evaluated before release. In order to survive in the wild, they must be able to fly and catch fish. (Shannon K. Jacobs)*

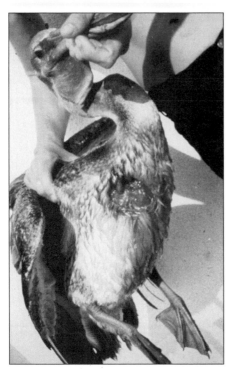

Hooked Bird. *This brown pelican, with an open wound in its chest, was snagged by a fish hook. If not treated, birds like this often die from infected wounds. (Stan Ashbrook)*

many healthy birds to declining wild flocks. For example, more than six hundred threatened brown pelican babies have been hatched by captive parents and eventually released.

Education Programs

Free education programs are offered at the sanctuary on the first Sunday of each month. The programs are presented by sanctuary staff, veterinarians, and other experts in their fields. Topics have included environmental awareness, bird identification, wildlife photography, and workshops for those who want to help rescue wild birds.

An ongoing education effort is teaching people how to help hooked birds. The 100,000 people who visit the place each year learn how to prevent hooking injuries.

"Amateur fishermen in Florida cause most of the injuries," Heath explained. "They aren't used to birds like brown pelicans that hang around people and dive for their food."

When brown pelicans catch a fish that has been hooked, the hook can snag them. Water birds also get caught in fishing line that people throw away or lose. The line can wrap around a leg or wing, trapping the bird. If the bird is able to fly, it usually gets tangled in branches. Many birds starve to death dangling from a tree.

The Peaceful Pelican

Pax was the first brown pelican hatched and reared in captivity by permanently crippled parents. Many ornithologists and other scientists said it couldn't be done, but Pax proved them wrong. It was a great day when the three-month-old pelican flew off to his freedom. But it was a sad day a few years later when a very sick Pax returned to the sanctuary on his own. Pax stuck his beak through slats in the gate where he had been raised. His parents

Snagged Bird. *Entangled in loose fishing line, a bird was caught in a tree and starved to death. (Stan Ashbrook)*

Baby Pax. *The first chick hatched by disabled brown pelican parents, Pax proved all the naysayers wrong. (Stan Ashbrook)*

still lived there. When volunteers let him in, Pax headed straight to the pen where he had been hatched. A band on his leg (worn by all pelicans hatched at the sanctuary) identified him.

Rehabilitators examined Pax and found a small fishing hook stuck in his back. Later that night the famous brown pelican died. A second hook was found puncturing his stomach wall. Like many other brown pelicans, Pax had swallowed a hook after grabbing a hooked fish.

Although Heath grieved for the pelican, he was pleased with Pax's life span. The brown pelican that was hatched in spite of his parents' handicaps lived an average number of years for a wild pelican.

Recyclers of the Sky

Vinnie, a black vulture, was hungry. When his sharp eyes spotted a dead opossum along the road, he banked to the right and soared low over a highway. A few hops later he was feasting on the body. Soon he had stuffed himself with opossum. When Vinnie heard the roar of a car, he jumped into the air for takeoff, but his body was too slow and heavy. The car's front fender slammed the vulture into a nearby tree. He landed with a dull thud. Later that day, when he was able to stand, he tried to fly, but his right wing would not work.

Vinnie's survival instinct told him that he had better find cover before he became somebody's dinner. He slowly hopped into bushes and hid. For the next week, Vinnie hobbled weakly around the bushes and slept a lot. Although the wing healed, the bones were not lined up correctly. He could fly only in short spurts with uneven flaps.

The last time Vinnie flew wild and free, he leaped into the air, trying to gain altitude and soar with outstretched wings, as he had done so many times before. But his wing was not strong enough. He crash-landed on grass. Suddenly Vinnie realized that humans who lived in the nearby house were approaching him. The black vulture hissed, swaying back and forth, warning them not to touch him.

The people notified Suncoast Seabird Sanctuary about the strange black bird. Volunteers arrived and captured Vinnie. Now a permanent resident at the sanctuary, Vinnie teaches people about the important role that scavengers play in nature, though he has to put up with a lot of prejudice because people associate vultures with death, disgusting meals, and bad smells (just imagine the smells we'd have to put up with if vultures *didn't* eat dead animals!). People also think vultures are dirty, but Vinnie proves them wrong again. He bathes and preens quite often. If vultures had dirty feathers, they would never be able to get off the ground, let alone soar beyond the sky.

According to rehabilitators, vultures have some interesting survival tricks. One is to vomit on whatever frightens them or tries to take their food. In another trick, designed to beat the summer heat, they splatter their droppings on their legs.

Black Vultures. *Some people think vultures are disgusting, but others appreciate how useful—and resourceful—the birds are. (They have some fascinating survival tricks.) (Shannon K. Jacobs)*

Wild Care, Inc.

Location: PO Box 760
Brewster, MA 02631-1760
508-896-2133
E-mail: wildcare@C4.net

Description: Home-based center treating native and migrating birds, mammals, and reptiles

Staff: Director Karen Von den Deale, 30 year-round volunteers, 70–90 baby bird volunteers (May through August)

Funding: Donations, memberships, fund-raisers

Newsletter: *Wild Times*, published twice a year

Programs: Yes

Tours: No

Wildlife rehabilitator Karen Von den Deale has been honored with a "Hero's Award" from the *Cape Cod Times* for her devotion to wild creatures and her contributions to Cape Cod. Von den Deale founded Wild Care in 1994 as the only full-time, full-service rehabilitation center on Cape Cod. In addition to treating native birds, mammals, and reptiles, Von den Deale

Early Birds. *Morning setup at Wild Care, Inc. All dishes are labeled with the animal to be fed and the food preparation. (Karen Von den Deale)*

cares for sick and injured birds that migrate along the Atlantic Coast flyway. In one year, Wild Care admitted eighty-seven different species.

Managing a busy wildlife clinic is a lot of work. To make the best use of her time, Von den Deale sends baby mammals to Wild Care's volunteers who are licensed rehabilitators in the area. (Baby mammals need to eat day *and* night, remember.) Some of the volunteers who help out year-round never come to the center at all—they work from their homes, handling Wild Care's twenty-four-hour telephone hotline and answering calls about injured wildlife or human-wildlife conflicts.

Wild Care receives hundreds of orphaned birds every year. To prepare for the mob, Von den Deale trains volunteers from the community to help in the center's baby bird nursery. During the spring and summer, seventy volunteers work in the baby bird nursery. Each volunteer works a three-hour shift once a week. Shifts start at 6 in the morning and end at 9 at night.

"You've got to feed insect-eating birds fifteen to sixteen hours a day, or they won't live," explained Von den Deale. "You can't just cover them up at 5 in the evening—they would be dead in the morning. So chickadees, nuthatches, and wrens are fed from dawn to dusk. Also, you have to make up different formulas for different species of birds. For example, finches don't eat what chickadees eat."

Education programs offered by Wild Care have included "Our Feathered Friends," describing the history, habits, behavior, and rehabilitation of local birds, and "House on My Back," detailing life cycles and survival needs of Cape Cod turtles.

Peninsula Considerations

Cape Cod is a peninsula, which means it has special advantages for wildlife rehabilitation because animals cannot get on or off the peninsula very easily. Therefore, they can be more easily controlled.

Cape Cod is one of the few places in the United States that does not have rabies, and the people of Massachusetts want it to stay rabies-free, so wildlife officials put out food that is baited with rabies vaccine. When animals eat it, they become immune to rabies.

"No rabies" is good news for Cape Cod rehabbers, who can treat rabies vector species such as raccoons, skunks, bats, and foxes. They still have to be careful, though, because there could always be the first case, possibly from a visiting dog or cat.

Puppet Mom. *A hand puppet, shaped like a great horned owl, is used to teach a baby owl how to eat. It helps prevent human imprinting. (Karen Von den Deale)*

A Ghoul of a Gull

One unusually cold winter on Cape Cod, a herring gull, found in a snowbank and brought to the center, was one of the harsh weather's victims.

"Everybody kept saying what a nice bird it was," Von den Deale said. "Well, you know you've got a sick or dead gull when it's nice!"

The skinny gull was so weak he could not stand up. Von den Deale tube-fed the gull, also treating him for parasites, but the gull did not improve. After three days with no progress, she decided to check the gull's blood, hoping for a diagnosis. Von den Deale had never had so much trouble drawing blood from a bird. When she tried to take blood from a vein in the wing, she couldn't get *any* blood. She clipped the gull's toenail (which usually causes bleeding), but got no blood there either. Finally a tiny bubble of blood appeared. Von den Deale smeared it onto a slide and rushed it to her veterinarian. The analysis results were shocking: the bird's white blood cells (which fight infections) were at *zero!*

Von den Deale asked the vet what that meant. "It means you have a dead gull," the vet said, "unless we try a blood transfusion."

Swapping Blood. *Rehabilitators Mary Capitummino (left, with sick gull) and Karen Von den Deale (right, holding Alby von Webb) head for the vet's office for a blood transfusion. (Karen Von den Deale)*

Alby von Webb and Brood. *"Alby teaches the babies how to chase the volunteers so they'll learn not to tolerate people,"* Karen said. *"When the babies are released, they're definitely wild birds."* (Karen Von den Deale)

Although Von den Deale had never participated in a bird blood transfusion before, she agreed. She volunteered two donors—a backyard chicken and Alby von Webb, a tame Toulouse goose. The vet told her to come back that afternoon with the gull and goose.

Alby von Webb is a foster mother at Wild Care who raises orphaned wild goslings. Now she had a new job—donating blood to a grumpy gull.

That afternoon, Von den Deale took the goose and gull to the vet's office. The vet drew some of Alby's blood and injected it into the gull. By evening the gull was preening. He finally had an appetite, so Von den Deale fed him liquid fish, and eventually whole fish and clams. Over the next week the bird got better. When the vet checked the gull's blood a week later, she found it had improved dramatically.

Von den Deale prepared to release the bird after he strengthened his wings for flying. Because the gull had received blood from a goose, Von den Deale gave him a fitting name—Gooul.

Bungee Crow

Crows are curious because they are smart birds—but sometimes that curiosity gets them in trouble. Such was the case when a young crow sitting in a pine tree spotted a piece of loose fishing line. He leaped into the air, flapped his glossy wings, and landed next to it. The crow pecked at the line, but it didn't move. A breeze blew the fishing line and wound it around the crow's leg like a boa constrictor. Disappointed that it wasn't food, the bird hopped into the air for takeoff. The line trailed after him.

All day the bird skipped around the grass, pecking at food containers people had dropped. When he flew into a nearby tree, the free end of the fishing line wrapped around a branch. Later, planning to raid an overturned garbage can, the crow jumped into the air, but he rose only a foot from the tree limb before he was jerked back by the line and slung upside down. The crow was strong. He flapped his wings until he could reach a branch with his beak and his free foot to pull himself upright. He pecked at the line that had tightened around his foot, but it didn't budge.

For several hours the crow leaped into the air, was snapped back, and dangled. Then he flapped himself back up to the branch, only to do it all over again. By the end of the first day the line had become tangled in his wing. By the second day, the weak crow was close to death. Still, he tried to get free.

People on the ground had watched the crow frantically trying to free himself in the tall pine tree. When they realized he could not get loose, they called Wild Care. A brave volunteer climbed the tree and rescued the dying crow. The bird was truly on his last leg when he was brought to the center. Von den Deale cut off the fishing line, cleaned up his leg wound, and let him rest. When he was strong enough to eat, she fed him.

It took a while, but the crow's wing healed well, and the bird was released. Curiosity cost the crow a serious injury. Hopefully it also taught him a valuable lesson in survival.

Curious Crow. After its rescue, the crow did well. It was released back to the wild. (Karen Von den Deale)

Birds of Prey Foundation

Location: 2290 S. 104th Street
                     Broomfield, CO 80020
                     303-460-0674
                     www.birds-of-prey.org
                     E-mail: raptor@birds-of-prey.org

Description: Large center treating more than 400 birds of prey yearly
Staff: 2 full-time, 1 part-time staff member; more than 50 volunteers
Funding: Donations, memberships, fund-raisers, thrift shop
Newsletter: Annual Christmas letter describing year's events and birds
Programs: School and community visits with education birds
Tours: No; annual open house for members and sponsors

Sigrid Ueblacker, founder and director of Birds of Prey Foundation, is described as a "true healer." She admits that she has always loved animals. "When I was a little girl in Austria," she said, "I didn't want to read until someone gave me a book about animals."

Ueblacker is known for her high professional standards as well as compassionate care, and she has created a rehabilitation center admired by many. Although BOP is not open to the public, Ueblacker occasionally schedules tours, and people from several countries have visited the center.

Ueblacker began rehabilitating raptors in 1981, starting in her backyard. At first she learned from a skilled wildlife veterinarian. Then she continued educating herself, studying and collecting books on raptors and taking courses in wildlife rehabilitation.

When she gives programs at schools and communities, Ueblacker likes to weave the natural history of birds into true stories.

A True Healer. *Sigrid Ueblacker uses forceps to feed a great horned owl that was injured when caught in a leghold trap. (Michael Judish)*

"I love having eye contact with a child with questions," Ueblacker said. "I love, too, the shadow programs, where a child comes to stay a day or a number of hours, following us around."

Roomy Flight Cages

Twenty-nine large flight cages at Birds of Prey Foundation are temporary homes for bald and golden eagles, falcons, hawks, and owls. The pleasant, sunny enclosures are filled with branches, ladders for climbing, trees, grass, and large pools for drinking and bathing. Because they are in such huge enclosures, birds are able to fly on their own anytime they want to, which gives them a lot of freedom to practice flying.

BOP rehabilitates about four hundred birds of prey each year. Volunteers donate thousands of hours to rescuing and rehabilitating the birds. They also do fund-raisers, clean cages, and raise live food sources—rabbits, quail, and mice.

Human Therapy

Humans sometimes are rehabilitated at BOP too—people who need to work off traffic violations by performing community service may apply at the center. A carefully selected few work about four thousand hours a year. These

Hawk Cage. *Birds of Prey Foundation has large raptor rehabilitation enclosures, allowing birds to exercise whenever they want. (Dave Felder)*

volunteers help with cleaning, building, and animal care. In fact, most of the foundation's intensive care unit was built through community service.

Few community volunteers leave the foundation without being touched by their experience. One man who had to work off one hundred hours was given the job of cleaning the rabbit hut. Within a month he had named all the rabbits.

"His probation officer wanted to know what we did to him because the man's attitude had changed so much," Ueblacker said. "The man used to complain all the time about his life. Suddenly he was announcing, 'At lunch today I saw a Swainson's hawk!'"

To Be or Not to Be—Free

Hamlet, a bald eagle, was very sick from lead poisoning when he was admitted to BOP. He probably had eaten an animal injured or killed with lead shot. Hungry raptors occasionally feed on roadkill or other carrion. They can be poisoned by lead pellets, lead sinkers, or poisons intentionally put out to kill wild creatures. BOP's veterinarian, Dr. Lee Eggleston, treated Hamlet for the lead poisoning. Ueblacker credits the veterinarian with saving the eagle's life.

Hamlet suffered from lead poisoning. (Trish Phillips)

Because Hamlet acted depressed and would not eat on his own, Ueblacker stayed with him over Christmas, putting off her family celebration. After many weeks of roller-coaster health, Hamlet began to improve. Soon Ueblacker moved him into a flight cage to practice his flying skills with other recovering eagles. At that point she stopped handling him.

"It was time to let go," she wrote in her newsletter. "This is the objective of our efforts: to care and to nurse when our wild birds need our help so desperately, and then to stand back quietly, watch their progress, and eventually return them to the homeland when they are ready to fend for themselves."

One warm, sunny day in December, 350 people gathered for the release of four bald eagles that had been rehabilitated at Birds of Prey Foundation. Hamlet was one of them. After a blessing ceremony given by a Native American medicine man, the four birds were set free to walk the wild winds.

Beautiful Blue Lady

Blue Lady, an endangered peregrine falcon, had not healed well at another rehabilitation center, so she was sent to BOP. Pneumonia had damaged the falcon's lungs, and her left wing drooped from an old fracture. No injured peregrine falcon had been returned to the wilds of Colorado in fifteen years. Would Blue Lady make it? Ueblacker gave her the best opportunity to heal. She placed Blue Lady in a large flight cage, reduced human contact, and fed her good falcon food. In response, Blue Lady practiced flying across the cage several times a day, strengthening her wings. To Ueblacker's delight, Blue Lady's wing soon straightened out.

Early that fall Ueblacker caught the falcon and put a numbered band on her leg, which meant that Blue Lady would be released. Ueblacker and Blue Lady traveled to the release site in a plane, flying together over the Rocky Mountains. Then they journeyed by car to the Colorado National Monument, where the injured bird had been found eight months before. Above a deep canyon, Ueblacker released the beautiful Blue Lady.

"She left my hands and disappeared below the rim of the canyon," Ueblacker wrote in her newsletter. "She turned into a ghostly blue shadow and became the hunter she once used to be. She cruised along the canyon walls as she flew from sunshine into shade."

Over the next few weeks, four sightings of her were reported. Thanks to Birds of Prey Foundation, Blue Lady once again graced the canyons. She made her home a hundred miles from the release site, where she has raised several nests of young.

Blue Lady. Would this beautiful, endangered bird make it? (Sigrid Ueblacker)

Canyon Cruisers. *A healed Blue Lady watches over her young. (Wendy Shattil and Bob Rozinski)*

9
Becoming Champions of the Wild

Wild Again. *A curious raccoon pauses to pose after release. (Critter Alley)*

Wildlife rehabilitators recommend the following twelve steps everyone can take to protect wildlife.

Take Responsibility for Pets

At least fifty million cats run loose in our towns, cities, and countrysides. If only 10 percent of these cats kill one bird a day, that still adds up to hundreds of millions of birds that die every year because of loose cats. They also kill more than a billion small mammals and reptiles a year.

Feline Killers. (*Greenwood Wildlife Rehabilitation Sanctuary*)

Cat attacks are the most preventable of all bird injuries and deaths.

How can responsible owners protect birds and small mammals? Keep cats inside. People do it all the time, and pets adjust. First, the cat should be neutered or spayed to reduce its urge to roam. Next, slowly cut back on the time the cat stays outside at night until it's not going out at all. It takes time, but cats (and people) can change. Your indoor cat will not be carrying pollen, dirt, and other worrisome things into your house, and will also have more energy since it won't be out stalking the streets at night.

The best part is the extra time you'll have with your cat. The average life span of a house cat is eighteen years. Outdoor cats live an average of only five years because of car hits, dog attacks, and diseases.

For specific information on how you can transform your outdoor cat into a happy indoor cat, see the box on the next page, "How to Make Your Outdoor Cat a Happy Indoor Cat," by Linda Winter, director of Cats Indoors! Campaign, American Bird Conservancy.

Dogs are a problem for wildlife too. When owners let their dogs run loose in city parks, open spaces, or wilderness areas, the dogs chase, harass, and kill wildlife. Young animals especially tend to get hurt.

If their owners are not careful about keeping them in a yard or house at night, dogs sneak off and join canine hunting packs. These packs terrorize and kill wild creatures—sometimes even those in zoos. We cannot blame dogs or cats for the hundreds of millions of wild animals they kill every year. Only owners, who are responsible for their pets, can stop this assault on wildlife.

How to Make Your Outdoor Cat a Happy Indoor Cat

By Linda Winter, director, Cats Indoors! American Bird Conservancy

Although it takes patience, an outdoor cat can be turned into a perfectly content indoor pet. The key is to make the conversion gradually and provide lots of attention and stimulation while the cat is indoors.

Cats are creatures of habit, so you must be careful to *slowly* replace your cat's old routine of going outside with the new routine of staying in. If your cat is outdoors most of the time, bring your cat inside for increasingly longer stays.

Gradually shorten the length of time the cat is outside until you no longer let him or her out at all.

Substitute outside excursions with periods of special play time. Supervised trips out on the patio can also make the transition from outside to inside a little easier. Cats need human companionship to be happy, and when they spend all their time out of doors, they get very little attention. An outdoor cat may welcome the indoors if he or she gets more love, attention, and play.

Provide plenty to keep your cat occupied indoors. Provide your cat with secure cat condos, which offer acceptable and interesting places to lounge, play, and scratch. You should also provide scratching posts, corrugated cardboard or sisal rope for your cat to scratch, and praise your cat for using them.

To encourage your ex-outdoor cat to exercise, offer interesting toys, especially those that are interactive. These usually consist of a long pole and attached line with fabric or feathers at the end of the line. Some cats enjoy searching for toys. If your cat likes to explore the house looking for "prey," hide his toys in various places so he can find them throughout the day. Be sure that the toys are not so small that they can be swallowed or get stuck in your cat's throat. Cats also enjoy ping-pong balls, paper bags, and cardboard boxes.

Provide your indoor cat with fresh greens. You can buy kits that include containers and seeds to grow, or plant pesticide-free alfalfa, grass, birdseed, or catnip in your own container. This way, your cat can graze safely and not destroy your house plants.

Your geographic location may affect your schedule of change; choose a good time of year to bring the cat indoors. In many parts of the country, the easiest time of year to make this conversion is prior to the cold winter months, when your cat is more likely to want to be inside anyway. By the end of winter, your cat may be completely content to remain inside.

If your cat remains stubbornly committed to life outdoors, help her adjust by providing an outdoor covered enclosure or run that the cat can access through a window or pet door. Such a facility gives the cat some of the advantages of being outside while minimizing the dangers. You can make the outdoor enclosure interesting and appealing by adding objects for the cat to explore, such as tree limbs, multilevel cat condos, tires, toys hanging from branches, and boxes in which the cat can curl up or hide. You can order a Cat Enclosure Kit, which measures 6′ × 6′ × 6′, for $249.95 plus postage and handling by calling toll-free: 1-888-554-PETS, or write: C & D Pet Products, 1663 Northstar Drive, Petaluma, CA 94954.

If you cannot or prefer not to offer your cat a run or enclosure, consider leash-training the cat so you can supervise her time outside. Attach the leash to a harness. Your cat may resist leash-training at first, but she will eventually accept the leash. Never leave your cat outside unsupervised while on a leash or lead.

Some cats may develop behavioral problems when they are no longer allowed outside. Most of these problems can be attributed to a change in routine that is too abrupt or lack of attention and stimulation inside. Review your steps and keep working with the cat. Be patient and continue to praise your cat when she plays with her toys, uses her scratching post, and does what she's supposed to do. If your cat becomes destructive or stops using the litter pan, consult a veterinarian or animal behaviorist to find ways to solve the problem. Remember that these symptoms can also be attributed to boredom and loneliness.

If you have just adopted a cat that stayed outdoors all the time, you should keep the cat inside from the beginning; otherwise, you run the risk of losing your cat. Using a long-range water pistol or a shake can when the cat asks to be let out is a very successful and harmless way to curb a cat from wanting to go outside. And don't forget to give your cat extra attention during the transition!

Additional tips for a happy indoor cat:

- Trim your cat's claws every one to two weeks to keep him from damaging furniture, rugs, and drapes, or glue on artificial nail caps called "Soft Paws" every six to eight weeks.
- Provide one litter pan per cat and scoop the litter pan at least once daily. With nonclumping litter, change once or twice weekly; with clumping litter, change every two to four weeks.
- Many cats enjoy the companionship of another cat or compatible dog of the opposite sex. If you can make the financial and emotional commitment, consider adopting another companion animal for yourself and for your cat.

(Adapted from "All Cats Should Be Indoor Cats" by Rhonda Lucas Donald, *Shelter Sense*, August 1990, and "From Outdoors to Indoors" by Karen Commings, *Cat Fancy*, September 1993.)

For more information, contact:
American Bird Conservancy
Cats Indoors! The Campaign for Safer Birds and Cats
1834 Jefferson Place NW
Washington, DC 20036
Phone: 202-452-1535; Fax: 202-452-1534;
E-mail: abc@abcbirds.org; website: www.abcbirds.org

Respect Wildlife Habitat

Are you aware of wild creatures when you hike or bike in the mountains, boat on a lake, or snowmobile in a forest? Do you think about their need for privacy and quiet? Just as we need to feel safe and secure in our homes, so wild creatures need peace and quiet. We have four walls to protect us, but wild animals depend completely on human consideration.

Being respectful of wildlife is especially important during nesting times. If adults raising their young are frightened off by loud or destructive human activity, they may become separated from their babies and abandon them. Stay on trails so animals have areas to themselves. When you see nests, keep a respectful distance away. Do not get too close to adults with their young.

Hunt and Shoot Responsibly

Hunters play important roles in protecting wild animals and habitats. Responsible hunters do not kill animals they don't plan to eat, and they don't shoot wildlife for target practice. Unfortunately, some irresponsible people have guns, and they shoot at anything that moves. Gunshot wounds are still a major source of injuries for bald eagles and other raptors.

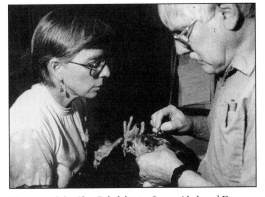

Shot out of the Sky. *Rehabilitator Susan Ahalt and Dr. Malcolm Blessing examine Memory, a bald eagle shot by a high-powered rifle. She survived but can't be released because of the injury. (B. D. Wehrfritz)*

The education eagle that Diana Shaffer of Wildlife Resqu Haus in Yorktown, Indiana, takes into classrooms lost a wing because someone filled it with buckshot. Shaffer reminds students what happens when someone carelessly shoots a wild creature.

"How would you like to spend your life in your room, not ever able to go out and play, ride on your bike with friends, or watch TV?" she asks. "That's what it is like for this eagle. She has to spend the rest of her life in a cage because someone shot her for fun."

Responsible hunters do not use lead shot. It has been banned in the United States because it causes lead poisoning. Many birds of prey are poisoned by lead because they eat animals that have been killed with lead shot. This problem often happens when the raptors are migrating and very hungry. Lead poisoning is fatal if not treated quickly.

Responsible hunters also report poachers (and others who destroy wildlife and habitat) to their state wildlife department or to a wildlife rehabilitator to keep spoilers from ruining the natural world for everyone else.

Fish Responsibly

Hooked Gull. *Fishermen can prevent hook injuries.* *(Karen Von den Deale)*

Lead fishing sinkers cause lead poisoning when water birds eat them. Responsible fishermen do not use lead sinkers. There are other choices—steel and nontoxic sinkers.

Fishing line is a major source of injury and death for threatened brown pelicans as well as other water birds. Responsible fishermen do not leave loose fishing line in lakes or oceans; they remove the line and dispose of it properly. Responsible fishermen do not cut the line if a bird gets hooked because the bird will become entangled in trees or bushes and starve, unable to get loose. There are other choices of fishing line besides monofilament. Some are made from cotton or other biodegradable fibers.

You can prevent hooking injuries by following these simple recommendations (adapted with permission from Suncoast Seabird Sanctuary):
- Before casting, make sure no water birds are flying above.
- If water birds are close by, wait a few minutes until they leave the area.
- Don't pull in a fish on a hook close to a bird; the bird will gobble it up.
- Never leave baited fishing tackle out in the open, unattended.
- Don't leave hooks hanging from the end of exposed fishing rods.
- Don't throw used fishing line or other plastic into the water.
- Don't feed water birds where people are fishing.

Boat Responsibly

Responsible boaters, water-skiers, and jet-skiers constantly look out for water birds, nesting birds, manatees, dolphins, and other water creatures. If any are spotted, they slow down and stay a respectful distance away. Responsible boaters stay away from marshy areas, where birds nest or hide; do not boat too close to islands; and do not speed around places where birds nest. Waves can drown young birds and drive off parents.

Drive Responsibly

It takes a lot of time for big birds to get into the air. Responsible drivers slow down in places where large birds hang out, including bridges and causeways. Drivers should also reduce their speed when they spot a large bird on the side of the road. It is probably eating roadkill. If birds see cars coming, they will fly toward an open area, and usually the closest such area is the middle of the road. When you see a bird by the road, give it time to take off, or you will hit it.

Many mammals are blinded by headlights. They often are hit by cars when crossing roads because they freeze when caught in car lights. Responsible drivers slow down in areas where these animals frequently cross.

Driving snowmobiles or motorcycles into wildlife habitat also requires attention. Stay on trails, and do not bother or chase wildlife.

Clean up Litter and Pollution

At least four million pieces of garbage, weighing 2.5 million pounds, are picked up along U.S. coastal shores every year. Think how much is *not* collected but ends up floating in the ocean or sinking to the bottom. What is the number-one coastal problem? Filtered cigarette butts. In addition, hundreds of thousands of plastic cups, lids, food bags, straws, bottles, and wrappers are picked up along beaches.

Trash looks like food to wild animals. They eat it and feed it to their young. Plastic bags look like jellyfish, a sea turtle delicacy. Many dead sea turtles have starved to death, their intestines filled with plastic.

Sick, stranded marine mammals have been found with plastic bags and balloons clogging their stomachs. Helium balloons can travel far when released, and they end up on land and in the sea. For this reason, some states have banned the release of helium balloons.

People can still enjoy helium balloons without endangering wildlife. One way is to use ceiling bags to catch the balloons after they are released. Another choice is to rent homing pigeons and release them all at once instead of using balloons at all. It is a more dramatic choice, and it is safer for wildlife.

Deadly Chokers. Cut up plastic sunglasses, four-pack and six-pack rings, bottle rings, and other plastic garbage before throwing away or recycling. They can be deadly for wildlife. (Critter Alley)

If six-pack or four-pack plastic rings or other plastic items are not cut up before being recycled or thrown away, they can become deadly chokers for wild animals. Every year rehabilitators admit ducks, raccoons, squirrels, seals, and opossums, among many others, that are trapped in plastic rings. Often the animals cannot be caught. Most starve to death because the tight rings prevent them from swallowing.

Think Before Feeding Wildlife

Feeding wild animals by hand is one of the worst things you can do because it makes wildlife too trusting of people—they expect food from everyone. Many people are afraid of wild creatures, and they become more frightened when approached by friendly wildlife. What do you think will happen to these animals? Hand-feeding wild animals is dangerous for people too. Wildlife are unpredictable. If you give peanuts to a squirrel, it might be fine one day, but the next day it might jump on you or bite your finger with its chisel-sharp teeth.

Don't Hand-Feed Wildlife. It's dangerous for you and for the animals, especially if they learn to trust people. (Shannon K. Jacobs)

Attracting Crowds

Some people put out food for wildlife because they think they are doing the animals a favor. Unfortunately, the food ends up attracting large numbers of creatures, and that is a dangerous situation for everyone. The more dense the wildlife population is, the more risk there is for disease. Animals fight more when crowded together, especially if food supplies dwindle or are stopped. When people stop feeding wild animals, some animals go hungry. Out of desperation, they may raid gardens, farms, or homes and become dangerous. Then angry people demand that wildlife officials kill the animals.

A Fed Fox Is a Dead Fox

In Kansas a man fed a fox every day for months. He taught the creature to scratch at his back door for food. Then the man went away on a trip, leaving the fox without a food source. The hungry fox ran all over the neighborhood, scratching on back doors, looking for food. When a frightened woman saw the fox at her back door, she thought it had rabies because it was not afraid of people. She called the state wildlife agency, and someone came out and shot the fox. The fox was tested and did not have rabies—it was just a hungry fox that had learned to trust people.

Chomper. Hand-fed regularly in a city park, Chomper bit twelve people before he was caught, rehabilitated, and released far away from people. (Urban Wildlife Rescue)

Don't Kidnap Wildlife

Wild animals belong in the wild. Captive creatures yearn for their freedom, and they never get over that yearning. It is wrong to cage these free spirits.

Wildlife Diseases

It is dangerous to keep wild animals in your home. Many carry zoonoses,

Open Pits. This young raccoon, attracted to a dumpster full of food, became trapped inside. The quick-thinking photographer placed a board inside, enabling the wayward coon to climb out. (Paula Stolebarger)

diseases that can be passed from wildlife to humans. Although wildlife rehabilitators know how to avoid zoonoses, the average person does not. Some zoonotic diseases can be fatal. In one (nonfatal) case, a woman picked up a young fox and took it home as a "pet." The fox played with the kids, cats, and dog. It hopped on the furniture and slept on the beds. But when the fox got sick and began losing its hair, the woman got worried. She took the animal to Operation WildLife in Linwood, Kansas.

While examining the fox, wildlife rehabilitator Diane Johnson noticed that the woman kept scratching herself. Hunks of hair fell out when the woman scratched her head. Johnson scraped some of the fox's skin and hair and looked at it under the microscope.

"This fox has mange," Johnson told the woman. "And so do you."

Mange is a skin disease caused by tiny mites that burrow under the skin. It often causes hair loss and can make animals sick enough to die. Although it is easily cured in humans, people can suffer from itching and hair loss. The fox had run all over the woman's house, infecting people and pets with mites. After leaving the fox with the rehabilitator, the woman and her family had to throw away their rugs, bedding, curtains, and carpeting.

Mange. *This young fox with mange infected a house when he was brought home as a "pet." (Diane Johnson)*

Wild Behaviors

Wild animals also have wild instincts and learned wild behaviors. One man's ignorance about this issue almost cost him dearly. When the man found a young coyote pup near its dead, car-hit mother, he took the coyote home because he thought it would be fun to keep it as a pet. The man expected the coyote to act like a tame, domestic dog. He fenced off the kitchen area for the pup. That area became the coyote's territory—the place where it ate and slept.

The man's three-year-old son loved to watch the pup. One day the little boy climbed over the gate to pet the "doggie" while the coyote was eating. The boy did not mean to, but he threatened the pup. Acting on instinct to protect its food and territory, the coyote lunged at the boy. The father grabbed his son just in time, saving him from being injured.

Was it the coyote's fault for behaving like the animal it was? The man finally admitted that he had made a mistake by taking a wild animal into his home. He took the pup to Johnson at Operation WildLife. Johnson taught the coyote how to be properly wild and later released it into the wild.

Dangerous Pets. *A coyote pup, taken home as a "pet," nearly attacked a man's young son. (Diane Johnson)*

Don't Buy Exotic Pets

With permits in certain states, it is legal to capture animals from the wild, breed them, and sell their young. Does being legal make it right? Wild animals never make good pets, even if born in captivity. All wild creatures have instincts they have no control over. As they get older, wild animals are driven by instincts to find a mate; protect their territory, food, and young; and stay alive. When they reach full size, these animals become uncontrollable, unpredictable, and dangerous.

What do people do with wild "pets" when the cute babies grow into snarling adults? Usually they lock them in cages or basements or turn them loose in the wild, unprepared to survive on their own. Sometimes people sell captive wild animals to game ranches. These places charge people to shoot the helpless animals for "sport."

Sad Wild "Pet" Story. *A woman had this cougar declawed as a kitten. But she had no decent place to keep him, so wildlife officials took the cat away from her. If a wildlife rehabilitator couple had not taken the cat, he would have been euthanized. The couple is now responsible for the care of this magnificent animal, who will spend the rest of his life caged. (Shannon K. Jacobs)*

Stolen. *This prairie dog was dug up in Texas and sold to a pet store in Florida. If people stopped buying wild animals, this wouldn't happen. (Shannon K. Jacobs)*

Wouldn't it be better to prevent such horrors and not make wild animals "pets" in the first place? Wild creatures never become "tame," no matter how affectionate they are when they're young. Wild animals' survival instincts tell them to fear and avoid humans. But if they are raised by people, they learn to trust us. This contradiction confuses them, and their behavior becomes even more unpredictable.

The best pets for families are domestic (bred to be tame) animals such as cats, dogs, hamsters, gerbils, and rabbits.

It took tens of thousands of years to domesticate wolves into the dogs we know today. Cats have been domesticated for only a few thousand years, and the difference shows—cats generally seem wilder than dogs, with stronger instincts.

Buying wild animals for pets encourages people to steal them from the wild. These animals are often kept in cruel conditions, and many don't survive long enough to be sold. For each wild animal that is bought, thousands more die from injuries, diseases, starvation, and the stress of being crammed into tiny, airless containers when they are used to being free.

Would you really want a wild "pet," knowing how dangerous, expensive, and miserable it will become?

Make Your Yard Wildlife Friendly

Pesticides Kill

Pesticides are designed to kill. They rarely kill just insects. Wildlife rehabilitator Elaine Thrune of Wild Again in St. Cloud, Minnesota, described a situation she has experienced several times:

A woman and her daughter bring in a sick bird. The little girl carries the bird in her hand. When she opens her fingers, the bird flips onto its back and twitches all over. Its eyelids flutter violently. Elaine has seen this behavior in other sick birds, so she knows what it is.

"Has anyone in your neighborhood sprayed their lawn with pesticides in the last few days?" Elaine asks.

The woman answers, "We had someone spray our lawn yesterday."

Elaine explains that the bird is acting as though it has been poisoned by pesticide spray.

"We did this?" the woman cries. "But the man who sprayed said it was perfectly safe. He didn't even wear boots."

Elaine suggests that the woman use nontoxic sprays on her lawn if she wants to stop poisoning birds. The woman shakes her head.

Pesticide Deformity. A young robin has a deformed beak because its mother was exposed to pesticides. (Critter Alley)

"I don't mind a few dandelions," she says, "but my husband insists on a perfect lawn."

Pesticides kill insects. What eats the poisoned insects? Birds. What eats birds poisoned by pesticides? Foxes, raptors, opossums, raccoons, snakes, and hawks. Sometimes cats and dogs eat them too.

Pesticides seep into our water supplies, rivers, and lakes. Who drinks the water?

There are many nonpoisonous products available. Check with experts at garden supply centers, botanical gardens, or wild bird centers. They will give you good advice about how to improve yards without poisoning all life-forms.

If you use a lawn service, ask the company for a list of your lawn problems and the chemicals being used to treat them. *Always insist on using the least toxic chemicals.*

And if you had the chance, wouldn't it be a great idea to give up 10 percent of your manicured lawn in exchange for an environment that is healthier for insects and other hungry creatures?

Planting for Wildlife

Did you know that hummingbirds and butterflies are attracted to certain plants? That specific trees are great for birds to nest in? That you can build

Hummingbird Garden. *Fourth grader John Weege in Littleton, Colorado, enjoys gardening for hummingbirds and butterflies because he gets to see them, identify them, and learn about them. (Shannon K. Jacobs)*

homes for bats? Planting and creating homes for wildlife help replace wild foods and shelters that are destroyed by development and provide wild creatures with food, water, cover, and places to raise their young. This is a more natural and effective way to provide food for wildlife than putting out food or hand-feeding them.

If you would like to learn more about planting for wildlife, look through books and videos in libraries, bookstores, and nature centers. Also contact the National Wildlife Federation (NWF) Backyard Wildlife Habitat Program (http://www.nwf.org/backyardwildlifehabitat/). NWF has given national certificates to more than twenty thousand such projects around the world created at homes, schools, and businesses.

Careful Mowing

It is a good idea to check your yard before mowing the grass. Some birds nest on the ground, and a few mammals nest in the grass, even near houses. Walk around the area and peek into the high grass. If you find a nest of rabbits or ground-nesting birds, consider waiting one or two weeks to mow until they are gone. If you cannot wait, call a wildlife rehabilitator and ask for advice.

Careful Tree Trimming

Unfortunately, most homeowners and tree companies trim trees in the springtime, right at the beginning of nesting season. Many baby birds and squirrels become orphaned or injured when trees are trimmed. Check tree branches before trimming. If you find nests with babies in them, call a wildlife rehabilitator before moving the nests. You can also help by banging on the tree a couple of times a day for a few days before the tree is trimmed or cut. That warns mother squirrels and raccoons to move their babies from the tree. For squirrels, this precaution should be taken in spring and fall because they give birth during both seasons.

Prevent Window Collisions

Experts estimate that ninety-five million birds are killed each year by hitting home or office windows. Why do birds smash into windows like kamikaze pilots? Because windows reflect trees and sky, which is where the birds need to fly to escape cats or raptors.

One of the big problems is that bird feeders, which attract birds, often are placed near windows so people can enjoy the birds. When birds are frightened by loud noises or the shadow of a real hawk, they do not have a good escape route.

If you are having problems with birds hitting your windows, try putting up hawk silhouettes, ribbons, or wind socks. You might also experiment with placing feeders in different places, either very close to or very far from windows. If feeders are placed about a foot away from windows, birds may not be able to gain enough takeoff speed to hurt themselves. Feeders hung in open areas, farther away from windows, allow birds to take off in all directions.

Feeding Fledgling. If birds are hitting your windows, try moving feeders closer to or farther away from the house. (Shannon K. Jacobs)

Wildproofing Your Home

Some people think the best way to handle an unwanted animal in the house or yard is to kill it. But that doesn't solve the problem. Find out what is attracting animals to your home. Is it food? Water? Shelter?

The best way to get rid of unwanted wild animals is to get rid of what attracts them. Here are some tips regarding how to do that:

- Take pet food inside at night. Remove the invitation to unwanted visitors.
- Put out enough bird seed for just one day. This discourages nocturnal prowlers—such as raccoons, skunks, and opossums—from raiding your bird feeder.

For the Birds? Bird food attracts other critters too. (Urban Wildlife Rescue)

- Store garbage in cans with tight lids; do not use just bags. If possible, keep trash in a closed garage or shed until collection day.
- Seal up cracks and holes in your house. Use heavy mesh wire to close up entry holes in the foundation, eaves, attic, or chimney or under porches. First make sure no animals (including birds) are trapped inside.
- Cover your chimney with a cap. Measure the chimney opening, take the measurements to your local hardware store, and ask for a chimney cap. Before installing the cap, make sure no animals (including birds) are trapped inside.

Encouraging Animals to Leave

If you have an unwanted animal resident, call a wildlife rehabilitator before you trap, poison, kill, or chase off the creature. Rehabilitators will give you sound advice on what to do and how to do it humanely.

During the spring many animals seek dark, quiet shelters where they can give birth and raise young. If an animal family is nesting in your house, try being patient for a few weeks. That is usually all it takes for the babies to be weaned. Then there are many more choices for you and the furry family. In the meantime, if the mother is chased off, trapped, or removed, the babies will starve.

Getting Rid of What Animals Like

The best way to evict wild creatures is to get rid of what they like—dark and quiet. Leaving a light on in an attic or chimney or under a porch can sometimes be enough to discourage the family.

Radios tuned to talk shows and turned up loud will drive off some creatures. Animals may get used to music (even bad music), but they do not like human voices. Stinky objects, such as rags soaked in ammonia and placed in the sleeping area, can send wild creatures running off. Wait until the babies are gone before you use any chemicals, though. Never use poisons or harmful chemicals. Who knows where they will end up? It might be in your cat's or dog's stomach.

Mix up the methods you use—smell, light, noise—so the animals don't get too used to any one method. They are, after all, very adaptable.

Be very careful of mothers with young. Never get between mothers and their babies. Most mothers will attack if they think their young are threatened. (See Chapter 11 for more specific information about handling wildlife conflicts.)

Fighter Moms. Don't get between a mother and her young. She may attack. (Urban Wildlife Rescue)

What Can Kids Do?

Learning About Nature

Kids have always had a special relationship with animals, and they can do a lot to help wildlife.

For kids, first ask yourself what you know about your wild neighbors. Can you name two mammals, two reptiles, and two birds living near you? It is much easier to care about something when you know its name.

Do you have a favorite native animal? Where does it live? What does it eat? Draw or photograph the animal, or write a poem about it. Learn all you can about the animal and its habitat, then work hard to protect both.

Share your knowledge with friends and family. All wild creatures, like all people, are fascinating. They can teach us amazing things. They deserve our attention and admiration.

Learning about nature means spending as much time as possible outdoors. You do not have to go far away to enjoy nature—just go *outside*.

Nature is a spider spinning a web in a corner of your porch.

Nature is a red-tailed hawk perched on a telephone pole, watching for prey.

Nature is a fox squirrel burying nuts in a city park.

Nature is a park, lake, or trees along city streets.

Nature is the desert, beach, or mountains.

Nature is your backyard.

Practicing the "Three L's"

Dr. John Huckabee, wildlife veterinarian for the Progressive Animal Welfare Society (PAWS) in Lynnwood, Washington, recommended three important ways to learn about wildlife. He called them "the Three L's"—look, learn, and leave alone.

"*Look* at animals and enjoy them, but from a distance," he suggested. "*Learn* all you can about wildlife from books, magazines, television programs, the Internet, videos, teachers, rehabilitators, or nature centers."

Huckabee added, "To *leave alone* means not to interfere with wildlife. Don't keep peeking into a bird's nest to see when the eggs will hatch. Don't take the nest home to see the eggs hatch."

Watching Feathered Friends

Can you name two birds that live in your neighborhood all year long? What about the names of two birds that migrate through your state?

Tracking Tadpoles. For nine-year-old Miquette Reardon, it's challenging and fun to catch and release tadpoles. (Shannon K. Jacobs)

There are 780 species of birds in North America. We are very lucky to have such a variety of feathered friends. Becoming a bird-watcher, or birder, is one of the easiest ways to begin learning about wildlife. Birds live everywhere.

Start by noticing the birds around your home. Listen to them. Spend a few minutes walking around your neighborhood or a nearby park, watching birds. Even common birds such as robins and crows are fun to observe. Notice their colors; their body size; the way they fly, walk, or hop. Listen to their many different songs.

Wildlife Groups

Join the Audubon Society, Sierra Club, or National Wildlife Federation, or check out other groups that offer field trips and classes. Many are offered through wild bird stores, such as Wild

Bird Centers and Wild Birds Unlimited. Also, natural history museums, botanical gardens, nature centers, and state parks provide classes and field trips. These are good places to meet other people who love to learn about wildlife.

Bird Books

When you begin to see differences in birds, you will be ready for a bird book. There are many kids' birding guides available. Check your library, local bookstores, or

Never Too Young. *A Rocky Mountain Bird Observatory volunteer shows four-year-old Erin Weber and Kyle, her younger brother, a banded migratory bird just before it's released. Groups like this are a great way to learn about birds and other wildlife. (Shannon K. Jacobs)*

Bird-Watchers. *Binoculars help these young bird-watchers identify common and rare birds that visit this city park. See the bird flying in front of the girls? The bird's baby, pictured in the next photograph, is hidden among cattails. (Shannon K. Jacobs)*

Baby Blackbird. *A fledgling red-winged blackbird hides among cattails, waiting to be fed by its parents. (Shannon K. Jacobs)*

Learning Is Caring. *Fifth grader Andrew Rork releases two garter snakes close to where he caught them. "They'll do better in the wild than in a cage in my house," Andrew explained. "They were refusing to eat, and the cage was too small for them." (Cindy Rork)*

bird centers. If you continue with your birding interest, you might want to save up for (or ask for, as a gift) binoculars to watch birds farther away.

Soon you will become an expert on birds. You can easily show off your knowledge because most people cannot identify birds very well. For example, while walking home from school one day, you might point out a winged wonder in the sky and casually say to friends, "Oh, look, a Swainson's hawk."

While everyone is gawking at the sky with open mouths, not seeing a thing, you calmly point to the black speck in the sky.

"Oh, my mistake," you say modestly. "It's a black vulture riding afternoon thermals, scouting for roadkill."

Learning Is Caring

Kids can do a lot to help wild creatures. Learning about your own native birds, reptiles, and mammals is an important first step. What you learn about, you will care about; what you care about, you will want to protect.

Nature Explorers. *Youngsters living on Lopez Island, Washington, visit a local beach and find—what—a huge octopus? Nope, just harmless kelp. The island adventurers are (left to right): Hillary Zoerb (age eleven), Emma Ewert (eight), Tasha Wilson (ten), Arielle Wilson (seven), Laurel Horn (twelve), Lilly Ewert (five), and Clara Ewert (two). (Greg Ewert)*

10
Handling Wildlife Conflicts

Hanging in There. *(Critter Alley)*

Is There a Skunk under Your Deck?

High Anxiety. *Penny Murphy shows a tree-company worker how to rescue a family of raccoons living in a tree that will be cut down. (Urban Wildlife Rescue)*

Bat House Humor. *A home for evicted bats, mounted on the side of a hair salon, is one of many bat houses in Mineral Wells, Texas. (Amanda Lollar)*

If there are bats in your attic or raccoons in the chimney, consider calling a wildlife rehabilitator to learn how to evict the animals without killing or harming them. "Pest" or animal-control companies may poison or trap (and kill) wild animals living in and around people's homes.

Rehabilitators can also suggest effective ways to prevent animals from entering your home in the first place. Prevention is a very important step to take, or more furred tenants will move in soon.

A good example of how rehabilitators teach their communities to positively handle wildlife conflicts is in Mineral Wells, Texas, where Amanda Lollar, director of Bat World Sanctuary, lives.

Lollar is a bat rehabilitator and an expert on Mexican free-tails (Texas's most common bat). She has designed bat houses specifically for these little creatures and has also taught local people how to put up the bat houses as alternative roosting sites. That way, when people evict the bats from vacant buildings and attics, the animals have somewhere to go.

Like most wild animals, bats are losing their habitat. Often the only shelters available to them are human structures. In the past, people killed bats that roosted inside homes and buildings. But the citizens of Mineral Wells know how to evict bat colonies *and* keep their bug-eating benefits. (One tiny bat can eat five hundred mosquitoes an hour!) People have mounted more than forty new bat houses in the town. These colorful (and sometimes humorous) houses provide habitat for thousands of Mexican free-tailed bats that desperately need homes.

Telephone Advice

Most rehabilitators give wildlife advice over the phone. They answer questions about wildlife behavior, offer options when human-wildlife conflicts occur, and refer callers to agencies that can help them. People sometimes call rehabilitators to report problems with wildlife; animals that are injured or orphaned; or incidents of abuse, neglect, or harassment of wildlife.

In one case a person called the Alabama Wildlife Rescue Service hotline to report a neighbor who was using a raccoon as live bait to train his hunting dogs. Knowing it was against Alabama state law to keep a raccoon without a permit, the hotline volunteer told staff members about the incident. The staff contacted a game

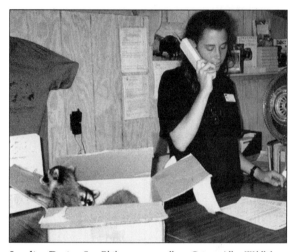

Juggling Duties. *Sue Philp answers calls at Critter Alley Wildlife Rehabilitation Center in Michigan. A box of orphaned raccoons waits to be admitted. (Critter Alley)*

warden, who confiscated the raccoon and took the animal to the rehabilitation center for treatment. It was released later, and the man who had kept the raccoon was prosecuted for illegal possession and abuse of a wild animal.

Volunteers all over the country give phone advice, handling hundreds of calls a year; saving money for individuals, private organizations, and the government; and preventing unnecessary suffering of animals.

Humane Solutions

When a landlord discovered a family of raccoons living in the attic of his apartment building, he called Jack Murphy at Urban Wildlife Rescue in

Aurora, Colorado. The renters and the landlord wanted the raccoons out of there, but they didn't want them hurt.

The landlord was lucky to find Jack Murphy and his wife, Penny, because they are experts at using humane solutions to solve wildlife conflicts. In a typical year the Murphys handle more than three thousand hotline calls and save at least eight thousand animals. (That number is in addition to the two hundred–plus injured and orphaned creatures they rehabilitate at their home-based center.)

Murphy explained to the landlord that raccoons (just like squirrels) usually have at least two dens. The solution was to make the mother feel unwelcome in the building so that she would pack up the babies and move to another den.

The landlord put a bright light in the attic and turned on a loud radio, as Murphy suggested. But the mother raccoon wouldn't budge. She was no fool— it was snowing outside, and the attic was warm and cozy. The landlord refused to harm the animals or dump them out in the cold. Instead, he continued to make a pest of himself, increasing the noise and light levels in the attic. Finally the weary raccoon mother packed up her babies and moved out one night.

Everyone benefited from the building owner's patience and kindness. The raccoon family stayed together, and many people learned about safe and caring choices when dealing with unwanted furry guests.

In another case, the person wasn't nearly as kind. When this homeowner found raccoons living in his chimney, he chased the mother away and dumped the six babies in a trash can. For two days the baby raccoons sweltered inside the metal can.

Someone heard about the heartless act and called Penny Murphy, who rescued the starving, frightened babies. If the homeowner had tried a humane solution, the mother raccoon would have moved her babies, and the problem would have been solved.

Instead, Penny and Jack Murphy had to become foster parents for the six orphaned

Supporting Wildlife. Penny Murphy operates a booth at Wild Oats Market, which was donating a portion of the day's sale to Urban Wildlife Rescue (UWR). Murphy answered many questions about UWR's services, which include advising people how to humanely evict wild creatures from their homes. (Urban Wildlife Rescue)

Saved from the Dump. If the homeowner who found this raccoon family had called a rehabilitator, he would have learned how to humanely evict the family, and the babies could have stayed with their mother. (Urban Wildlife Rescue)

raccoons. This meant a lot of work and expense for the Murphys, who had many other wild babies to care for. However, the raccoon kits were lucky. With the nurturing care they received at Urban Wildlife Rescue, they grew into healthy wild animals. As soon as the raccoons were old enough to survive on their own, the Murphys returned them to the wild.

Wildlife Care Basics for Veterinarians

The following information was excerpted with permission from *Wildlife Care Basics for Veterinary Hospitals: Before the Rehabilitator Arrives,* written by Irene Ruth in cooperation with The Fund for Animals. Irene Ruth, a Connecticut wildlife rehabilitator, wrote this invaluable manual after receiving numerous calls over the years from veterinary offices requesting information on how to temporarily care for and treat injured and orphaned wildlife. (To order copies of the complete manual, contact Becca DeWeerdt (becca@fund.org) at The Fund for Animals, www.fund.org, Phone: 203-389-4411, Fax: 203-389-5544.

Immediate Care for Wild Animals until You Contact a Rehabilitator

Many wild animals that come into a wildlife rehabilitator's care are first taken to veterinarians' offices. Because the care of wildlife can be very different from the care that you would routinely give to domestic animals, we can help you by supplying some vital information and suggestions.

While it is commonly understood that a veterinarian may take in wildlife and provide emergency care, it is illegal for a veterinarian or veterinary technician to do long-term care of the wild animal unless he or she has obtained a state and/or federal rehabilitator's permit. The only exceptions are pigeons, European starlings, English sparrows, mute swans, monk parakeets and game species such as wild turkeys, ring-neck pheasants and bobwhite quails. For these birds, you do not need a permit.

If you are a veterinarian or veterinary technician interested in working with a rehabilitator, contact your state wildlife agency for a directory of rehabilitators in your area

Get a Name and Phone Number Before You Talk to the Finder

Your first contact with the "finder" of wildlife in distress is usually over the phone. Phone advice can solve problems, save lives, and prevent orphaning and kidnapping of wild animal babies.

If your office is busy and you can't spend time on the phone dealing with this sort of problem, please give the caller The Fund for Animals' Hotline: 203-389-4411, and website: www.fund.org. Also, give the caller the names and phone numbers of several rehabilitators in the area, if you have them, and explain that these wildlife experts will give them the best advice. To obtain a list of licensed rehabilitators in your state, contact your state's fish and game agency and ask for the department in charge of licensing wildlife rehabilitators.

Often a finder will call a veterinarian's office to get information about raising wild animal babies. Please do not give out any information that would make a person feel that he or she is qualified to raise them. If callers have wildlife in their possession, have them bring the animals to you or to a rehabilitator immediately.

If the finder seems determined to raise a wild baby, first be sure to ask for a name and phone number. Then explain that formulas are very specific to each species and must be changed continually as the animal grows so that it is receiving the proper nutrition. Tell them that the wrong foods can keep an animal alive and it may even look fine, but the bones and teeth will be weak, and the internal organs will not develop well. The animal will have a difficult life, if it even survives. Explain that a wild animal baby that is sweet and cuddly now will grow up to be an adult wild animal with strong defense and survival instincts. A wild animal will be unhappy in captivity and will be a potential danger to humans and domestic animals.

As a last resort, explain that it is illegal for the public to keep wildlife except to rescue and transport to a licensed rehabilitator or veterinarian.

Keeping the animal could involve a heavy fine, and the animals may be confiscated and destroyed.

The Basics: Getting Information from the Finder

It just takes a few minutes to get this information, and some of it will help you decide what treatment will be needed next.

- Name, address, and phone number of the finder
- Where the animal was found (specifically, what town, and in what context—under a tree, in the road, etc.
- If it is a baby, does the finder have any idea what happened to the mother? (See Chapter 10 in this book, "If You Find Orphaned or Injured Animals," to help you determine if the animal really needs help.)
- When was it found?
- What has happened since then?
- Has it been fed? If so, what and how much?
- Who has handled the animal? How often?
- Were gloves worn? (This is an important question to ask about mammals, and especially about rabies vector species.)
- Was there any possibility of a cat attack? If so, time is of the essence. Since cats have extremely toxic bacteria in their saliva that will quickly bring on septicemia, an antibiotic should be administered as soon as possible.

Once the Animal Arrives at Your Facility

Some veterinary offices have the staff, time and facilities to do a complete exam and initial emergency care for wild animals, including giving antibiotics and fluid therapy and doing wound care and parasite removal. Some do not. If your office does not, we absolutely understand and appreciate your taking the animal in and performing the basics.

Emergency medical care for wildlife is basically the same as for any animal. The physical exam, however, may be trickier. Prey species, such as birds and rabbits, may appear tame and quiet. This is instinctual behavior for animals when hurt, to avoid attracting predators. The animals may be experiencing tremendous stress. Being held captive can cause enough stress to be life threatening; birds and rabbits can literally die of fright.

Sometimes it is necessary to do an exam in several parts, placing an animal back into its cage and allowing it to calm down before proceeding. Open-mouth breathing in birds can be a sign of stress. Intense struggling, screaming, and crying should also tell you a mammal needs to take a break. Sometimes the hand-on exam is not practical, as in the case of an adult mammal or raptor. It may be that the best that can be done is a visual exam.

Move slowly and speak softly. Keep movements, noise, and especially talking, to a minimum. Make no direct eye contact with the animal, as this may be seen as threatening. Avoid strong smelling soaps or perfumes. The exam and the confinement of the animal should be done in the quietest part of your facility.

Cold metal exam tables add to the animal's stress during the physical exam. Place a soft cloth or blanket on the table first. If a towel is used, be sure that there aren't any loops or loose threads that can snag claws and wings. T-shirts, sweatshirts, fleece or baby blankets are ideal. Have more cloths handy to help manage the animal. Cloths can be used to wrap around the animal to hold it securely while being examined or to cover its eyes. This will help calm down the animal. Never leave a wild animal unattended during an examination or treatment.

Protect yourself and the animal by wearing gloves at all times. Wear rubber gloves when handling *any* wild mammal. Use thick leather gloves for all adult mammals, older juvenile mammals, and big birds. Keep your fingers out of the tip of the gloves. Protect your eyes and neck from birds with long sharp beaks. If you have not had your rabies pre-exposure vaccines yet, please get them as soon as possible.

As soon as the emergency care and stabilization has been done, a rehabilitator should be contacted and the animal transferred to that rehabilitator.

The Fund for Animals

Urban Wildlife

Following is a description of The Fund for Animals' Urban Wildlife program, a very comprehensive source of information regarding current and humane solutions for solving wildlife conflicts.

Founded in 1967 by the prominent author and animal advocate Cleveland Amory, The Fund for Animals is one of the largest and most active nonprofit organizations working for the cause of animals throughout the world.

The Fund for Animals' Wildlife Rehabilitation Center, established in 1983 in southern California, is a leading medical center for native wildlife such as bobcats, coyotes, and raptors.

The Urban Wildlife program is among the many educational services offered by The Fund (www.fund.org/urbanwildlife/). Several excellent "Coexisting with Wildlife Fact Sheets," written by Director Laura Simon, can be downloaded from the site. We have included a few of these in Appendix B.

In addition, there is a hotline that anyone can call, which gives free advice on how to handle problems concerning orphaned, injured, and "nuisance" wild animals. It's a Connecticut number, so the call will be long distance if you don't live in the state. The number is 203-389-4411.

Here is background information from The Fund for Animals' Urban Wildlife program:

> Every day people and wild animals are forced into closer and closer contact. A farm is turned into a housing development. A few acres of woods become an industrial park. Wildlife habitat gives way to urban sprawl.
>
> But to our surprise, many of the former residents do not run away. They adapt with great resourcefulness to their new circumstances. The result is a rising number of conflicts between people and wildlife, particularly during the spring and summer birthing season when wild animals take advantage of any cavity and food source that help them raise their young.
>
> For years the only answer has been to trap the "offending" animal. However, trapping is inhumane and often results in orphaned young being left behind. To make matters worse, the vacated niche is quickly filled by other animals from the surrounding area. The Fund for Animals provides a public service by offering effective, humane, innovative, long-term solutions that solve wildlife problems at their source.
>
> If you need help solving a wildlife problem in your home or community, please call The Fund for Animals' Urban Wildlife Hotline. We work seven days a week to give free advice for solving injured, orphaned, and "nuisance" wildlife situations, whether it's a family of raccoons denning in the chimney, a baby bird fallen from the nest, or a baby skunk wandering into a restaurant. We also help communities and politicians come up with humane, effective, long-term solutions to more broad scale problems, such as increasing numbers of resident complaints about Canada geese, pigeons, or skunk odor. We help communities better understand urban wildlife, dispel myths and exaggerated fears that residents may hold, and teach people how to coexist with the wildlife that shares their habitat.

Cottontail with Dandelion. *This rabbit is big enough to be on his own and capable of fending for himself without the help of humans. Originally, the cottontail was kidnapped by a well-meaning but misinformed human who thought it was an orphan. It was released three days after admission. The photo shows a representative size of what is considered releasable. (Diane Johnson)*

In Good Hands. *A young burrowing owl will get proper care at Birds of Prey Foundation. (Michael Judish)*

Appendix A:

If You Find Orphaned or Injured Animals

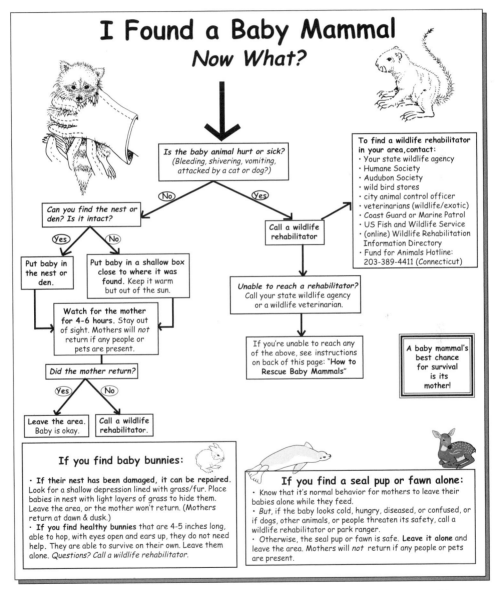

I Found a Baby Mammal
Now What?

Is the baby animal hurt or sick?
(Bleeding, shivering, vomiting, attacked by a cat or dog?)

No / **Yes**

To find a wildlife rehabilitator in your area, contact:
· Your state wildlife agency
· Humane Society
· Audubon Society
· wild bird stores
· city animal control officer
· veterinarians (wildlife/exotic)
· Coast Guard or Marine Patrol
· US Fish and Wildlife Service
· (online) Wildlife Rehabilitation Information Directory
· Fund for Animals Hotline: 203-389-4411 (Connecticut)

Can you find the nest or den? Is it intact?

Yes / **No**

Call a wildlife rehabilitator

Put baby in the nest or den.

Put baby in a shallow box close to where it was found. Keep it warm but out of the sun.

Watch for the mother for 4-6 hours. Stay out of sight. Mothers will *not* return if any people or pets are present.

Unable to reach a rehabilitator? Call your state wildlife agency or a wildlife veterinarian.

Did the mother return?

Yes / **No**

If you're unable to reach any of the above, see instructions on back of this page: **"How to Rescue Baby Mammals"**

A baby mammal's best chance for survival is its mother!

Leave the area. Baby is okay.

Call a wildlife rehabilitator.

If you find baby bunnies:

· **If their nest has been damaged, it can be repaired.** Look for a shallow depression lined with grass/fur. Place babies in nest with light layers of grass to hide them. Leave the area, or the mother won't return. (Mothers return at dawn & dusk.)
· **If you find healthy bunnies** that are 4-5 inches long, able to hop, with eyes open and ears up, they do not need help. They are able to survive on their own. Leave them alone. *Questions? Call a wildlife rehabilitator.*

If you find a seal pup or fawn alone:

· Know that it's normal behavior for mothers to leave their babies alone while they feed.
· *But*, if the baby looks cold, hungry, diseased, or confused, or if dogs, other animals, or people threaten its safety, call a wildlife rehabilitator or park ranger.
· Otherwise, the seal pup or fawn is safe. **Leave it alone** and leave the area. Mothers will *not* return if any people or pets are present.

How to Rescue Baby Mammals

(Only adults should rescue baby mammals. Before rescuing adult animals, seek guidance from a wildlife rehabilitator.)

1. **Prepare a container.** Place a soft cloth on the bottom of a cardboard box or cat/dog carrier with a lid. If it doesn't have air holes, make some. For smaller animals, you can use a paper sack with air holes punched in.
2. **Protect yourself.** Wear gloves, if possible. Some animals may bite or scratch to protect themselves, even if sick; wild animals commonly have parasites (fleas, lice, ticks) and carry diseases.
3. **Cover the animal with a light sheet or towel.**
4. **Gently pick up the animal and put it in the prepared container.**
5. **Warm the animal if it's cold out or if the animal is chilled.** Put one end of the container on a heating pad set on low. Or fill a zip-top plastic bag, plastic soft drink container with a screw lid, or a rubber glove with hot water; wrap warm container with cloth, and put it next to the animal. Make sure the container doesn't leak, or the animal will get wet and chilled.
6. **Tape the box shut or roll the top of the paper bag closed.**
7. **Note exactly where you found the animal.** This will be very important for release.
8. **Keep the animal in a warm, dark, quiet place.**
    Don't give it food or water.
    Leave it alone; don't handle or bother it.
    Keep children and pets away.
9. **Contact a wildlife rehabilitator, state wildlife agency, or wildlife veterinarian as soon as possible.**
    Don't keep the animal at your home longer than necessary.
    Keep the animal in a container; don't let it loose in your house or car.
10. **Wash your hands after contact with the animal.**
    Wash anything the animal was in contact with — towel, jacket, blanket, pet carrier — to prevent the spread of diseases and/or parasites to you or your pets.
11. **Take the animal to a wildlife rehabilitator as soon as possible.**

> It's against the law in most states to keep
> wild animals if you don't have permits,
> even if you plan to release them.

I Found a Baby Bird
Now What?

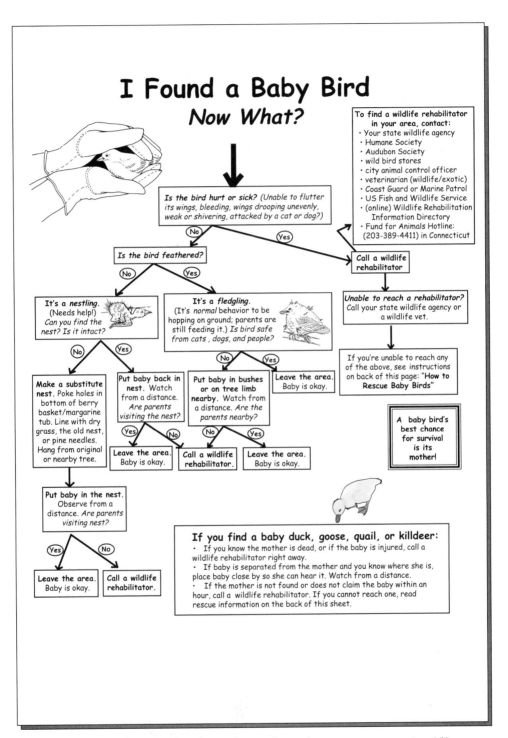

To find a wildlife rehabilitator in your area, contact:
- Your state wildlife agency
- Humane Society
- Audubon Society
- wild bird stores
- city animal control officer
- veterinarian (wildlife/exotic)
- Coast Guard or Marine Patrol
- US Fish and Wildlife Service
- (online) Wildlife Rehabilitation Information Directory
- Fund for Animals Hotline: (203-389-4411) in Connecticut

Is the bird hurt or sick? *(Unable to flutter its wings, bleeding, wings drooping unevenly, weak or shivering, attacked by a cat or dog?)*

No → Yes →

Is the bird feathered?

No → Yes →

Call a wildlife rehabilitator

It's a nestling. (Needs help!) Can you find the nest? Is it intact?

It's a fledgling. (It's *normal* behavior to be hopping on ground; parents are still feeding it.) Is bird safe from cats, dogs, and people?

Unable to reach a rehabilitator? Call your state wildlife agency or a wildlife vet.

No → Yes →

No → Yes →

If you're unable to reach any of the above, see instructions on back of this page: "**How to Rescue Baby Birds**"

Make a substitute nest. Poke holes in bottom of berry basket/margarine tub. Line with dry grass, the old nest, or pine needles. Hang from original or nearby tree.

Put baby back in nest. Watch from a distance. *Are parents visiting the nest?*

Put baby in bushes or on tree limb nearby. Watch from a distance. *Are the parents nearby?*

Leave the area. Baby is okay.

A baby bird's best chance for survival is its mother!

Yes → No →

No → Yes →

Leave the area. Baby is okay.

Call a wildlife rehabilitator.

Leave the area. Baby is okay.

Put baby in the nest. Observe from a distance. Are parents visiting nest?

Yes → No →

Leave the area. Baby is okay.

Call a wildlife rehabilitator.

If you find a baby duck, goose, quail, or killdeer:
- If you know the mother is dead, or if the baby is injured, call a wildlife rehabilitator right away.
- If baby is separated from the mother and you know where she is, place baby close by so she can hear it. Watch from a distance.
- If the mother is not found or does not claim the baby within an hour, call a wildlife rehabilitator. If you cannot reach one, read rescue information on the back of this sheet.

How to Rescue Baby Birds

(Only adults should rescue baby birds. Before rescuing adult birds, seek guidance from a wildlife rehabilitator.)

1. **Prepare a container.** Place a clean, soft cloth with no strings or loops on the bottom of a cardboard box or cat/dog carrier with a lid. If it doesn't have air holes, make some. For smaller birds, you can use a paper sack with air holes.
2. **Protect yourself.** Wear gloves, if possible. Some birds may stab with their beaks, slice with their *talons* (claws) or slap with their wings to protect themselves, even if sick; birds commonly have parasites (fleas, lice, ticks) and carry diseases.
3. **Cover the bird with a light sheet or towel.**
4. **Gently pick up the bird and put it in the prepared container.**
5. **Warm the bird if it's cold out or if the bird is chilled.** Put one end of the bird's container on a heating pad set on low. Or fill a zip-top plastic bag, plastic soft drink container with a screw lid, or a rubber glove with hot water; wrap the warm container with cloth, and put next to the bird. Make sure the container doesn't leak, or the bird will get wet and chilled.
6. **Tape the box shut or roll the top of the paper bag closed.**
7. **Note exactly where you found the bird.** This will be very important for release.
8. **Keep the bird in a warm, dark, quiet place.**
   Don't give the bird food or water.
   Leave the bird alone; don't handle or bother it.
   Keep children and pets away.
9. **Contact a wildlife rehabilitator, state wildlife agency, or wildlife veterinarian as soon as possible.**
   Don't keep the bird at your home longer than necessary.
   Keep the bird in a container; don't let it loose in your house or car.
10. **Wash your hands after contact with the bird.**
    Wash anything the bird was in contact with — towel, jacket, blanket, pet carrier, to prevent spread of diseases and/or parasites to you or your pets.
11. **Get the bird to a wildlife rehabilitator as soon as possible.**

> It's against the law in most states to keep
> wild animals if you don't have permits,
> even if you plan to release them.

Helping Marine Animals

Who Should Help?

Only experts should assist or rescue marine animals. These animals have very special needs, and they are too unpredictable for untrained people to manage.

If you see an orphaned, stranded, injured, or dead marine animal (manatee, dolphin, whale, sea turtle, seal, sea lion, or otter), *call the state Marine Patrol or Coast Guard right away.*

What to Report to Officials

· *When* you saw it (time of day)
· *Where* it was located
· *How* it appeared (stranded, injured, etc.)

Dead marine animals should also be reported so biologists can check on the cause and, possibly, prevent more deaths.

Healers of the Wild, Shannon K. Jacobs. Johnson Books, 2003.

Appendix B:

Coexisting with Wildlife Fact Sheets

Fund Facts: Coexisting with Wildlife Fact Sheet #1

Bats in Your Belfry? Humane Ways to Solve Wildlife Problems

Wild animals often nest or roam near human dwellings, especially during the spring or summer when they seek out cavities to begin nursing and raising their young. Here is some practical advice on how to resolve common wildlife problems using humane and inexpensive methods.

BATS

Q: What should I do if there's a bat in my house or there are bats roosting in my attic?

A: Don't panic. Bats have been plagued by centuries of superstitions, but they are actually one of nature's more gentle creatures. If you are positive that the bat has not bitten anyone or been in anyone's bedroom overnight, confine the animal to one room and open a window or exterior door. The flying bat will locate the opening by echolocation. All you need to do is turn out the lights, stand in a corner, and you should see the bat fly out. If the bat is not flying, check draperies or other places where the bat can hang easily. Wear heavy gloves and capture the bat either by placing a shoebox over the bat and then gently sliding a piece of cardboard underneath, or by carefully putting a towel over the bat and carrying the bat outside for release (put the bat on a wall or tree limb; they cannot fly up from the ground). Avoid direct contact with the bat so you don't get bitten. If the bat has bitten someone, contact your local health department for instructions and contain the bat for rabies testing, if possible.

Bats enter buildings through holes under roof overhangs, in eaves, vents, cracks around windows, through spaces under ill-fitting boards, and around pipes leading into the house. They can squeeze through openings as small as a dime-sized hole, so when the bats are gone make sure to repair or patch all entry points, which are usually dis-

cernible by oily stains. To locate bat entry holes, watch at dusk to see where the bats fly out from. Do *not* patch any holes from May to September or you may entrap flightless juvenile bats inside! Please refer to this site for bat exclusion methods: www.batcon.org.

BEARS

Q: How can I stop bears from getting into my trash can or birdfeeder?

A: Treat bears with respect and give them distance. If you live near bear habitat and you don't want bears on your property, you should not put out a birdfeeder. Bears are attracted to any type of food left outdoors. You can prevent them from coming near your property by storing all food indoors and all trash in airtight garbage cans. You can order bearproof garbage cans and food storage lockers from McClintock Metal Fabricators (800-350-3588 or www.mcclintockmetal.com).

BEAVERS

Q: Beavers in my neighborhood are chewing on trees and building dams that flood roads. What can I do?

A: First, tell your local officials that killing beavers and destroying dams will not solve the problem—migrating beavers will move in and build a new dam. Instead, certain measures such as wrapping hardware cloth around tree bases to prevent felling, or installing perforated PVC or flex pipes through beaver dams to control flooding, are very effective ways to resolve beaver problems. Any state wildlife agency can get free "beaver baffler" materials for landowners through the U.S. Fish and Wildlife Service's "Partners for Wildlife" program (call the Branch of Habitat Restoration at 703-358-2201 to locate your state coordinator to find out about this little-known program). Please contact our campaign office (301-585-2591) for our video and brochure on "A New Way to Solve Beaver Problems." The Fund for Animals also provides a hotline specifically for beaver conflict questions at 203-389-4411.

BIRDS

Q: A baby bird fell from the nest and I touched him. Will the parents reject their chick now?

A: It's a myth that birds abandon their chicks if a person touches them. Unlike other animals, birds are not sensitive to human scent. Just put the baby birds back in their nest. If the original nest was destroyed, hang a wicker or woven stick basket close to where the original nest was. (These are the kinds of baskets that flower arrangements come in. They can be purchased inexpensively at supermarket florist departments or garden stores. Many people have them around the house.) Woven stick baskets make perfect substitute nests, and they allow rain to pass through so the birds don't drown. You should watch for an hour to make sure the parents return to the new nest to feed their chicks. If they don't return, or the chicks have no feathers, call your wildlife agency to locate the nearest wildlife rehabilitator.

Q: A bird keeps attacking my window! What's going on?

A: Male birds commonly attack windows during mating season. The bird wrongly assumes that his own reflection is a rival in his territory! You can prevent this by hanging squares of aluminum foil outside the window to break up the reflection or Post-it notes all over the inside of the window.

Q: Pigeons, starlings, or sparrows are roosting on my building. How do I get them to leave?

A: Roosting birds' droppings can be annoying to people. Poisoning is extremely cruel (the intent of some common poisons is to cause extended seizures in birds and supposedly frighten other birds away) and does not solve the problem because other birds will soon move in to fill that vacancy. A better solution is to modify the habitat, which encourages them to go elsewhere. While a flat ledge is attractive to pigeons, a false ledge can be made by placing a board at an angle of at least 45 degrees so that birds will slide off when they land. You can also use bird netting or a stretched-out, nailed-down "Slinky" from a toy store, to make sure birds will not land on your ledges, rafters, or other horizontal surfaces. If you use a

Slinky, stretch it so two fingers fit between the spirals. The Bird Barrier Company specializes in humane bird exclusion devices (call 800-503-5444 for a free catalog or visit www.birdbarrier.com). If bird mites come through the air conditioner, get rid of them by using a mite spray from a pet store.

COYOTES

Q: There are coyotes in my neighborhood and I'm afraid they'll attack my children or pets. What should I do?

A: Coyotes are generally afraid of people, and rarely attack humans. The best thing you can do for cats and small dogs is to keep them indoors—both for their own safety and for the safety of neighboring wildlife. Coyotes are opportunistic eaters, and are attracted to places where they can find "easy pickings" of fruit, trash, or small animals such as mice and rats, etc. You can make sure you don't attract coyotes to your house by taking several additional precautions: (1) don't keep pet food outdoors, (2) pick the fruit from your trees as soon as it ripens and keep rotten fruit off the ground, and (3) keep trash can lids securely fastened and keep trash cans in your garage until collection day.

DEER

Q: If I find a fawn alone, does that mean the fawn is orphaned?

A: People mistakenly assume that a fawn is orphaned if found alone. Rest assured that the mother is nearby. The doe will only visit and nurse her fawn a few times a day to avoid attracting predators. At four weeks old, the fawn will begin to travel with the mother. Just leave the fawn alone unless (1) you *know* the mother is dead, (2) the fawn keeps bleating, or (3) it is lying on his side. Mother deer are wary of human smells. If you have handled the fawn, rub an old towel in the grass and wipe the fawn to remove human scent. Using gloves, return the fawn to exactly where he or she was found.

Q: How can I stop deer from eating shrubs and flowers in my garden?

A: There are several good deer repellents, such as "Big Game Repellent Deer Away," which is available at garden stores. An 8-foot woven wire fence or high-tensile electric wire fence kit (available at many garden stores) will keep deer away from small gardens if installed properly. The Fund for Animals offers a brochure called "Living With Deer" that describes in detail many of these fencing techniques, effective repellents, and lists more than 100 types of plants—including marigolds, daffodils, and hydrangeas—that deer generally find unpalatable and will stay away from. To request a free copy of "Living With Deer" please call our campaign office (301-585-2591) or visit our website (www.fund.org).

GEESE

Q: How can I stop geese from defecating on my lawn?

A: Go to your local party store and buy several helium-filled Mylar balloons with weights at the bottom. Set them around your yard—their reflectiveness and bobbing movement will scare the birds away. For information on "Rejex-It," a grape-flavored goose repellent, call the Bird Barrier Company at 800-503-5444. A new multisensory repellent called "Flight Control" combines a sense of digestive upset with a UV-colored warning system. When applied to grass, it is visible to the geese but not to humans. For other long-term humane solutions to geese-human conflicts, contact Geese Peace (www.GeesePeace.org).

GOPHERS AND WOODCHUCKS

Q: What can I do to prevent gophers and woodchucks from eating the tender roots of plants I've just planted?

A: Before planting, make a fine-meshed chicken-wire basket around the root ball of your plant. Or line your garden with a 3-foot-high floppy chicken-wire fence, which will bend backwards if the woodchuck tries to climb it. Create an L-shaped barrier by sinking hardware cloth 6 inches into the ground and then bend it at a 90-degree angle *away from* the garden for another 12 inches to create a "false bottom," so they can't dig under the barrier.

MICE AND RATS

Q: How do I rid my house or apartment of mice or rats?

A: You can prevent mice and rats from coming into your home by sealing all holes and small openings (rodents can enter buildings through holes no bigger than 1/2 inch in diameter) with caulking, steel wool, or cement. Use hardware cloth to patch larger holes and to screen all vent openings. Also, it is crucial to store food in secure containers and to make sure lids fit tightly so that you don't attract rodents. If you have mice or rats in your home,

you can order catch-and-release traps from the Tomahawk Live Trap Company (800-272-8727 or www.Livetrap.com) and then release the rodents far away from your home. You must then follow up by rodent-proofing your home or the problem will recur. To catch multiple mice easily, put a 55-gallon garbage can partially under the kitchen counter and put cheese pieces, sunflower seeds, peanut butter mounds, and lids of water inside the can. The mice will walk on the counter, jump into the can, but not be able to climb out.

MOLES

Q: How can I stop moles from tunneling in my yard?

A: The best solution is a new, environmentally friendly repellent called "Mole-Med," which is available at hardware and garden supply stores or by calling the company directly (800-255-2527). Mole-Med is made of emulsified castor oil and will last one to two months per application, but you should reapply it after heavy rains. Pesticides are never recommended for mole control as they are toxic to humans and domestic animals as well as wildlife.

OPOSSUMS

Q: What should I do if I find a dead opossum on the road?

A: Wearing gloves, you can move the dead animal off the road. If it's spring or summer, check to see if the opossum is a female and if there are live babies still in her pouch or in the immediate area. If found, call your state wildlife agency to locate a wildlife rehabilitator immediately.

RABBITS

Q: What should I do if I find (or my lawn-mower hits) a nest of baby rabbits?

A: If the nest is intact, leave it alone! Mother rabbits visit their young only two or three times a day to avoid attracting predators. If the nest has been disturbed, or if you have reason to believe that the babies are orphaned, you can put an "X" of yarn or sticks over the nest to assess if the mother returns to nurse her young. If the "X" is moved by the next day, the mother has returned to nurse them. If the "X" remains undisturbed for 24 hours, call your wildlife agency to locate a rehabilitator. Keep all cats out of the area because they will surely find and kill the helpless young rabbits. Don't touch the babies (unless orphaned) because mother rabbits are very sensitive to foreign smells and may abandon their young.

Q: What should I do if my cat caught a baby rabbit (or bird)?

A: Unfortunately, scientific studies show that one of the biggest killers of baby rabbits and birds is free-roaming cats. If the rabbit or bird appears unharmed, put the animal back where found and keep your cats indoors. Luckily, rabbits are fully weaned by the time they're only three weeks old and the size of a chipmunk! If you must relocate an older rabbit, use a lawn or field that has brush or other cover nearby.

Look very carefully for puncture wounds, which can be almost imperceptible. If the rabbit or bird has any puncture wounds, bring the animal to a veterinarian or rehabilitator quickly. Cats have toxic bacteria in their mouths, which become lethal unless the victim is put on antibiotics immediately. You can save more wild animals just by keeping your cats indoors. Remember that in the spring and summer, wild animals have helpless babies on the ground where cats can get them. If you absolutely can't keep your cats indoors, you can use multiple-bell collars, which will alert some wild animals to your cats' presence. Also consider purchasing the Cat-Fence-In System, which is a unique, humane barrier that keeps cats from climbing over fences or up trees (for ordering information, call 702-359-4574). Pet supply stores sell a variety of breakaway collars—purchase two additional large bells (sold separately with S-hooks) and attach them to the cat's collar. The bell on most collars is too quiet to do much good, and stealthy cats learn how to keep it still. Therefore, you need two large bells per collar.

RACCOONS

Q: What should I do if raccoons den in my chimney or attic?

A: In spring and summer, mother raccoons may use chimneys and attics as denning sites for raising their cubs. The best solution is to wait a few weeks for the raccoons to move out on their own, which they will do when the cubs are big enough to go on outings. Raccoons rarely create any smell or mess—mother raccoons clean their babies meticulously to avoid attracting predators. Once the raccoons are gone, promptly call a chimney sweep to install a mesh chimney cap (or seal any holes leading to the attic) and this situation will never occur again.

If you must evict a raccoon family, remember that raccoons look for a quiet, dark, and nonnoxious-smelling place to raise their young. By creating the opposite conditions, you can encourage them to leave sooner if absolutely necessary. For chimney raccoons, place a blaring radio (all-night rock or rap stations) in the fireplace. Then put a bowl of ammonia on a footstool, just under the damper. For attic raccoons, leave all the lights on and place a blaring radio and some rags sprinkled with 1/4 cup of ammonia around the attic. Apply these deterrents at dusk *only*; even harassed mother raccoons will try to avoid moving their young in daylight. Be sure to get a chimney cap installed once they're gone or this situation will occur again soon. Remember—the only permanent solution is to seal all entry holes once the animals have left.

Q: There's a raccoon in my yard during the daytime. Is the raccoon rabid?

A: Even though raccoons are nocturnal, mother raccoons sometimes forage during the day when they have nursing cubs depleting their energy. Cat food and garbage left outside will attract raccoons to an area. Only if an adult raccoon seen in the daytime is showing abnormal behavior such as paralysis, unprovoked aggression, moving in circles, self-mutilation, making screeching sounds, or showing supreme tameness should you call your local animal control officer or police department and keep people and companion animals away.

Q: What can I do to stop raccoons from continuously knocking over my garbage cans?

A: Overflowing or uncovered garbage cans provide an open invitation for hungry raccoons. The simplest solution is to put out your garbage cans for pickup in the morning, after the nocturnal raccoons have returned to their dens. If you must put out your garbage cans at night, try building a simple wooden box outside and storing your garbage cans in it. For easy access, the top should be hinged and have a latch in front secured with a snap hook. A third option is to get a good plastic garbage can with a 4-inch-high, *twist-on* lid, such as the kind made by Rubbermaid. Keep the can upright by wrapping bungee cords around the middle and securing it to an upright object.

SKUNKS

Q: How do I get a skunk out of my garage?

A: Skunks commonly wander into open garages when the door is left open. Just open the garage door before dark. Skunks have terrible eyesight, so as long as you move slowly and quietly, the skunk will hardly notice you. Leave a 2-foot band of flour across the outside of the garage and watch for footprints to confirm that the skunk has left. To neutralize any unpleasant odor, a nontoxic deodorizer called "Odors Away" can be purchased at hardware stores for approximately $4.

Q: There's a skunk in my window well. Why doesn't he jump out?

A: Skunks are not good climbers. They often fall into window wells and can't get out. If the window well is shallow, put a piece of wood in the window well (at a less-than-45-degree angle) to serve as a plank so the skunk can walk out. If the window well is deep, put on gloves and place smelly cat food or cheese in the far corner of a pet carrier or rectangular garbage can (tipped on its side) and slowly lower it into the window well. The skunk will be attracted to the food and will walk into it. Then slowly raise the carrier or can to ground level, elevator-style, and let the skunk stroll out. Skunks have terrible eyesight and will not spray you if you move slowly and talk soothingly to them. Remember, skunks also give a warning by stamping their front feet, which gives you a chance to back off! Most importantly, purchase or make a window well cover out of mesh so this situation doesn't recur.

SQUIRRELS

Q: What should I do if a squirrel has fallen down my chimney?

A: Squirrels commonly fall down chimneys and can't get out. Hang a 3/4-inch-thick rope or long branch down the chimney (securely fastened at the top) so the squirrel can climb out. Then be sure to put a chimney cap on the flue to prevent recurrence. Chimney caps will also prevent squirrels from building shallow nests at the top of the flue, which may make it dysfunctional or a fire hazard in winter. A second option, if the fireplace can be sealed off, is to set a live box trap in the fireplace baited with bread and peanut butter, and open the damper so the squirrel comes down. Check frequently to see when the squirrel goes into the trap and release him outside immediately. Be sure to have a chimney cap installed so this situation doesn't recur.

Q: What if squirrels are nesting in my attic?

A: If the squirrels are in your attic and it's baby season (spring, late summer, or early fall), chances are good that you have a mother with young. Try to find the nest so you can monitor it. Wait a few weeks until the squirrels leave on their own, or wait until they're fully furred and mobile, and then apply a one-way door over the entry hole. You can make a one-way door or purchase one from Tomahawk (800-272-8727). Once you are certain the squirrels have left, seal the entry hole permanently with hardware cloth. You can spray Miller's Hot Sauce (to order call 800-233-2040) onto the hardware cloth to deter them from trying to chew back in. To prevent access to your roof, trim any overhanging tree branches. You can also put a 3-foot band of sheet metal at least 6 feet above ground, around the base of any tree, to prevent squirrels from climbing up—but first make sure there are no active nests in the tree!

Q: How do I stop squirrels from eating all my bird seed?

A: You may have a difficult time keeping the nimble squirrel away from a free buffet. You can contact your local nature center or Audubon Society, or specialty bird stores, for a good baffler design for a free-standing feeder, or purchase the "Absolute" bird feeder, which has a lever that closes off the bird seed when a heavy animal like a squirrel lands on it. Another newly designed battery-operated bird feeder, "The Yankee Flipper," twirls fast when a squirrel lands on it, literally flipping it off. We strongly discourage the use of any capsaicin-based "hot pepper" powder mix, which, although advertised as a "humane" repellent when mixed with bird seed, reportedly makes squirrels quite sick and can be irritating to birds' eyes as well as to the humans who handle it.

THE PROBLEM WITH TRAPPING

Q: Should I call a wildlife nuisance control operator to trap animals who are bothering me?

A: We advise against trapping unless there's an immediate threat to you, your family, or your companion animals. When animals nest in your attic, chimney, or basement, the best strategy is to give the animals a grace period (especially a mother with young) or, if absolutely necessary, place deterrents such as ammonia-sprinkled rags, a blaring radio, mothballs in socks, or bright lights around the nesting area to encourage their departure. Then find all entry holes and seal them with hardware cloth. Live trapping is very traumatic for wildlife. There are people now in the business of removing "nuisance" animals for pay, yet we have concerns about the killing methods used by many of them, such as drowning an animal. If you must hire a nuisance wildlife control person, we recommend that you find someone who gives you a written guarantee that he will (1) use nonlethal methods only, (2) release the animals together (so juveniles aren't separated from their mothers) and release them on-site (relocated animals have low survival rates when released in unfamiliar areas), and (3) do the necessary exclusion and repair work to prevent wild animals from entering your home. Ask the right questions so you don't pay hundreds of dollars for an inhumane "solution."

If you have a wildlife problem that is not addressed in this fact sheet, please call The Fund for Animals' Urban Wildlife Hotline at 203-393-1050.

WILDLIFE HELP ON THE WEB

Bat Conservation International
www.batcon.org

Beavers: Wetlands & Wildlife
www.telenet.net/users/beavers

Bird Barrier
www.birdbarrier.com

Cat Claw
www.catclaw.com

Deerbusters
www.deerbusters.com

Deer-Resistant Landscape Nursery
www.deerresistantplants.com
www.flightcontrol.com

Flock Fighters USA
www.flockfighters.com

Geese Peace
www.GeesePeace.org

Living With Deer
www.fund.org/library

McClintock Metal Fabricators
www.mcclintockmetal.com

A New Way to Solve Beaver Problems
www.fund.org/library

Scarecrow
www.scatmat.com/scarecro2.htm

Strieter-Lite Wildlife Reflectors
www.strieter-lite.com

Tomahawk Live Trap Company
www.Livetrap.com

Written by Laura Simon,
Urban Wildlife Director

The Fund for Animals • 200 W. 57th St., New York, NY 10019 • (212) 246-2096 • FAX: (212) 246-2633 • www.fund.org

Solving Urban Duck Problems

Each year, people are amazed to see ducks and ducklings in the most unlikely places, such as walking single-file through city streets or nesting under bank-teller windows! Luckily, ducklings are precocious and mature quickly. Here are some commonsense solutions to typical problems encountered in suburban and urban settings.

Q: There's a duck nesting in the worst place! What should I do?

A: Ducks commonly nest in poor spots, such as under bank-teller windows or the middle of busy ball fields. These nests may fall prey to cats, dogs, or human malice. However, moving the eggs and nest is not only illegal according to federal law, but also the parents usually won't follow it. We suggest putting up educational signs and perhaps trying to fence off the nest temporarily. There isn't much else you can do. Some people have tried moving the nest, a few feet at a time, into a better area. This may work if the relocation site is nearby and you move the nest bit by bit. However, the mother may stay on the nest, making relocation impossible. It's usually best to leave the nest alone and hope for the best.

Q: Ducklings were separated from their mother. Is there a way to reunite them?

A: If the mother was seen recently, wait it out for an hour and see if she comes back. If the ducklings are beginning to scatter, or you're not sure how long they've been alone, put a plastic laundry basket over them, upside down, to contain them while waiting for the mother to return. She will see them through the lattice sides of the basket and make contact. If she returns, slowly approach and overturn the basket so she can collect her young.

Q: A duck family has taken over my pool! How do I get them to leave?

A: The best solution is to leave them alone, as long as the ducklings are able to get out of the pool. The mother will move her young when they are older and less vulnerable. If you must evict them, go to your local party store and buy silver Mylar balloons with heavy weights on the bottom. Put the balloons around the perimeter of the entire pool, about every 20 feet. The balloons will bob in the breeze and make the ducks nervous. To enhance the harassment effect, you can also float a

beach ball in the pool or use an electric boat. There's a product called a "Scare-Eye" balloon, which has giant reflective eyes (for an enhanced scare effect) and is available at most hardware or garden stores or through mail order via Bird Barrier, Inc. (800-503-5444 or www.birdbarrier.com).

Q: There's a duckling stuck in my pool! How do I get him out?

A: Most ducklings get stuck in pools because the water level is too low. The solution is to either raise the water level (simplest approach), fish it out with a net, or create a ramp angled less than 45 degrees, with a wet towel attached to it for traction.

Q: I'm afraid the duckling I see is orphaned.

A: If you know where the duckling came from, then it's best to take the duckling to that pond for release. The duckling will soon rejoin his family. Sometimes other ducks will even foster-parent the young duckling. If the duckling was left behind for a while and his origin is unknown (e.g. fished out of a storm drain or spillway), you can contain the duckling with an upside-down laundry basket (as described previously) and monitor to see if the mother returns. If she doesn't come back after four to eight hours, call your local fish and game agency to locate a wildlife rehabilitator. These are tough judgment calls. If you need to hold the duckling(s) in captivity for a few hours, *do not* give them water to swim in because ducklings are not waterproof until they're older. They may become chilled and die. Just give them a shallow pan of water (to drink) and some crushed, nonsugary cereal like Cheerios.

Q: How do I move a duck family out of a contained courtyard?

A: You can shepherd them out by creating a "moving wall," namely having people hold sheets between them and move behind the ducks, forcing them to walk in the desired direction. However, consider waiting to move them out because the young may be vulnerable. Sometimes we encourage the temporary feeding of greens like kale, spinach, and also poultry starter food (available from an animal feed store) and setting up a shallow kiddie pool with ramps, until the ducklings can fly. We encourage provisioning particularly in cities, where early eviction can mean certain death.

Q: How do I catch and move a duck family if absolutely necessary for their safety?

A: The only way to catch adult ducks is to do so at night (they don't see well in darkness). Creep up on them while they sleep, then gently cover them with a lightweight blanket or towel, and scoop them into a carrier. Catch the ducklings next with a net or sheet, but try to minimize stress, as they will be scared and may scatter. Be sure the net doesn't have large holes through which they may escape or become entangled. Consult your state fish and game agency prior to any intervention for any special authorization you might need.

Q: Ducklings fell through a sewer grate! How do I get them out?

A: These are tricky situations. Often you'll have to contact your town's Public Works Department for assistance with removing the grate. The police can be a valuable resource in terms of help-ing you contact the correct town employee. You'll need a fishing net or a fabric "hammock" stretched between two golf clubs to catch the ducklings below the grate. You may have to be creative in terms of capture strategies, depending on the logis-tics of where they're stuck. Once you catch them, make sure they are dry (or use a hair dryer) before setting them back outside for the mother to re-trieve. Put an upside-down laundry basket over them until the mother comes (so they don't scat-ter), and then slowly lift it when she reappears. If she doesn't come back by nightfall, contact your local wildlife rehabilitator.

Written by Laura Simon,
Urban Wildlife Director

The Fund for Animals • 200 W. 57th St., New York, NY 10019 • (212) 246-2096 • FAX: (212) 246-2633 • www.fund.org

Solving Racoon Problems

Raccoons are intelligent, fascinating, and highly adaptable mammals. As we destroy more and more wildlife habitat, we force animals like raccoons to come into closer contact with us. There's no need to panic or pay hundreds of dollars for trapping services because most problems can be easily resolved with some simple advice and household materials. Many conflicts occur in spring and summer when raccoons take advantage of cavities in human dwellings to raise their young. This is why it's vital to solve problems in a way that doesn't separate a mother from her cubs. Here are some solutions to common raccoon problems:

Q: How do I keep raccoons out of my garbage?

A: Overflowing or uncovered garbage cans provide an open invitation to hungry raccoons. The simplest solution is to put out your garbage cans for pickup in the morning, after the nocturnal raccoons have returned to their dens. If you must put out your garbage cans at night, get the kind of plastic garbage can with a tall (4-inch high) *twist-on* lid, which raccoons can't open. Another option is to build a simple wooden box outside for storing garbage cans. For easy access, the top should be hinged and have a latch in front secured with a snap hook.

Q: I found raccoons in my dumpster—how do I get them out?

A: Often garbage disposal companies don't close dumpster lids after emptying them in the early morning hours. Raccoons are enticed by the food smells, jump in, and can't climb the slippery sides. This problem is easily resolved by putting some strong branches or planklike pieces of wood in the dumpster so the raccoons can climb out. If your company leaves dumpster lids open all the time, we strongly recommend posting a sign telling employees that it's vital to keep the lid closed so animals don't become trapped inside.

Q: There's a raccoon in my yard but it's daytime—does that mean the animal is rabid?

A: Even though raccoons are considered nocturnal, mother raccoons sometimes nap in trees or forage during the day when they have nursing cubs, which deplete their energy. Coastal raccoons take advantage of the tides and are *often* seen by day. Call your local animal control officer or police if an adult raccoon seen in daytime is acting at all sick or *showing abnormal behavior* such as partial paralysis, circling, staggering as if drunk or disoriented, self-mutilating, screeching, or exhibiting unprovoked aggression or unnatural tameness. Otherwise just leave the raccoon alone and keep people and pets away from the animal.

Q: How do I get raccoons out of my attic or chimney?

A: In spring and summer, mother raccoons often take advantage of chimneys and attics as denning sites for raising cubs. The easiest and best solution is to wait a few weeks for the raccoons to move out on their own. As soon as the cubs are old enough to go on nighttime outings with their mother, she will take them out of the chimney once and for all rather than continually carry them back and forth. Remember that mother raccoons clean their babies meticulously to avoid attracting predators. If you absolutely must evict the raccoon family, remember that raccoons look for quiet, dark, and non-noxious-smelling places to raise their young. By creating the opposite conditions, you can evict them using the following methods.

Eviction of chimney raccoons: Keep the damper closed and put a blaring radio (rock or rap music works best) in the fireplace. Then put a bowl of ammonia on a footstool near the damper. Apply these deterrents *just before dusk*; mother raccoons won't want to move their cubs in broad daylight. Be patient; it may take a few days for the mother to move her young. Once you inspect and make sure all the raccoons are gone, promptly call a chimney sweep to install a mesh chimney cap (the best kind has a stainless-steel top) and this situation will not recur.

Eviction of attic raccoons: Leave all the lights on and place a blaring radio and rags sprinkled with 1/4 cup of ammonia around the attic. You can also enhance the deterrent effect by adding cayenne pepper or the commercial repellent Repel™ around the attic or by hanging an electrician's drop light over the denning area. Apply these deterrents *just before dusk*; mother raccoons will not want to move their cubs in daylight. Be patient;

it may take a few days for the mother to move her young. Once the raccoons are gone* promptly seal any entry hole and this situation will not recur.

Q: Raccoons keep eating the food I put outdoors for the cats!

A: If you leave food out all the time, you will attract raccoons and other animals. The solution is to feed the cats only at a certain time in the morning or midday, then take away any uneaten food. The cats will get used to the schedule and modify their behavior accordingly.

Q: A raccoon keeps coming through my cat door and eating all the cat food!

A: No self-respecting raccoon is going to ignore a free buffet! The best solution is to feed your cats indoors and not use a cat door at all. There are strong, electrically controlled doors that you can purchase that only let your designated pet in. You can call RC Steele at 800-872-3773 for more information on the Electronic Dog Door (item LA30-2296).

Q: I put in a Japanese pond but the raccoons are eating all the fish!

A: It is difficult to have a delicacy like fish in an area and expect raccoons not to take notice! The best solution is to maintain a higher water level (at least 3 feet deep) and stack cinder blocks, large rocks, or ceramic pipes in the bottom of the pond so the fish can escape from the raccoons and take refuge.

Q: Raccoons keep making a mess of my lawn. How do I stop this?

A: The raccoons are going after the grubs in your lawn. If you keep your lawn well watered, this exacerbates the problem since it drives the grubs to the surface layer of the soil. The good news is that the grubbing activity, although unsightly, does not permanently damage the lawn. A long-term, ecological solution is to apply the product "Milky Spore" to the soil. This natural bacteria will spread and get rid of the grubs, but it takes a long time to work (one year or more). We don't recommend

chemical pesticides due to their toxic effect on the environment, people, and animals.

Q: Raccoons keep getting into my chicken coop!

A: The only answer is to reinforce your chicken coop so the raccoons cannot have access to the chickens. Heavy-gauge welded wire should be used and another layer of finer mesh put over it to prevent raccoons from being able to reach through. Although an inconvenience, once an animal pen is well reinforced and maintained, there will be no more problems.

Q: Why not just trap the raccoon (or hire a trapper) to solve the nuisance problem?

A: Trapping is rarely a solution to wildlife nuisance problems. As one animal is removed, another from the surrounding area will soon take his place. The answer is to exclude the animal from the food or nesting source that is attracting him. Nuisance wildlife control companies charge a fee—sometimes hundreds of dollars—for problems that homeowners can often resolve themselves. In addition, when animals are trapped during birthing seson, starving babies may be left behind. Homeowners are then horrified to find a foul odor emanating throughout their house. Animals should never be trapped under extreme conditions, such as on sunny rooftops, in rain, snow, sleet, or other bad weather, which will cause the animals to suffer and die.

We *discourage trapping* unless an animal is stuck somewhere and can't get out or poses an immediate threat to humans or domestic animals. If you do hire a nuisance trapper, be sure to read our "Standards for Working with a Nuisance Wildlife Control Operator" brochure first to ensure that humane practices are followed and no animals are orphaned in the process.

Written by Laura Simon,
Urban Wildlife Director

The Fund for Animals • 200 W. 57th St., New York, NY 10019 • (212) 246-2096 • FAX: (212) 246-2633 • www.fund.org

---

*Most attics contain clutter, making it hard to verify if the raccoons are gone. Before sealing any entry hole, stuff it first with newspaper and see if the paper stays in place for three successive nights. If so, the den is vacated. After sealing the entry hole with hardware cloth, make sure no raccoons are left behind by leaving a sardine or marsh-mallows in the attic and checking if the food is uneaten after 24 hours, or sprinkle flour in front of the entry hole and check for footprints of a raccoon trying to get out.

Solving Woodchuck Problems

Woodchucks are harmless, comical vegetarians who are commonly sighted in suburban backyards and along roadways. Conflicts usually arise over who gets to eat the garden vegetables! Suburban landscapes provide perfect habitat for woodchucks. Our raised decks provide cover and a perfect place to raise young, and our lush lawns provide a virtual buffet. Most woodchuck conflicts occur in spring and summer, just when birthing season has begun. That's why problems need to be solved in a way that doesn't leave orphaned young behind.

Q: How do I keep a woodchuck out of my garden?

A: The best way to exclude woodchucks is by putting up a simple chicken-wire or mesh fence. All you need is a roll of 4-foot-high chicken wire and some wooden stakes. Once the job is done, it won't matter how many woodchucks are in the neighborhood because they won't be getting into your garden!

There are two secrets for making a successful fence:

Tip #1: The top portion of the fence needs to be only 2-1/2 to 3 feet high but it should be staked so that it's wobbly—the mesh should not be pulled tight between the stakes; rather there should be some "give" so that when the woodchuck tries to climb the fence, it will wobble, which will discourage him. Then he'll try to dig under the fence, so ...

Tip #2: Extend your mesh fence 4 inches straight down into the ground and then bend it and extend the final 8–12 inches outward, away from the garden, in an "L" shape, which creates a false bottom (you can also put this mesh "flap" on top of the ground, but be sure to secure it firmly with landscaping staples or the woodchuck will go under it). When the woodchuck digs down and hits this mesh flap, he'll think he can't dig any farther and give up. It won't occur to him to stand back a foot and *then* start digging!

If you aren't willing to put up a fence, you can also try the following scare techniques, which do work in some cases:

1. Line your garden with helium-filled, silver Mylar balloons, or make a low fence made of twisted, reflective Mylar tape bought at your local party store. Be sure to purchase heavier weights to attach to the bottom of the balloons. The balloons bobbing in the wind will scare the woodchucks.

2. Put blood meal fertilizer* around the perimeter of your garden, sprinkle cayenne pepper around the plants, and spray your plants with a taste repellent such as Ropel™ (available at garden stores) every two weeks.

Q: There's a woodchuck under my shed. How do I get him out?

A: Woodchucks don't undermine foundations and really aren't likely to damage your shed. In spring and summer, the woodchuck under your shed is probably a mother nursing her young, which is why we encourage you to consider leaving them alone. Be sure you really need to evict the woodchuck before taking action. If you must, put some dirty kitty litter down the woodchuck burrow—the urinated part acts as a predator odor, which often causes the entire family to leave. Ammonia-sprinkled rags or sweaty-smelling socks placed in the burrow may also cause self-eviction.

Q: I am afraid the woodchuck will hurt my children!

A: Woodchucks are harmless vegetarians who flee when scared. Remember that even a small child looks like a giant predator to the woodchuck. There is no cause for alarm—woodchucks live under houses and day care centers all over the country—and healthy woodchucks simply don't attack children or pets. If chased, woodchucks will quickly flee to their burrows.

Q: I see a woodchuck circling and falling over—is he rabid?

A: Woodchucks have a higher susceptibility to rabies than other rodents, yet the incidence of rabies in woodchucks is still very low. Woodchucks are much more susceptible to the roundworm brain parasite, which causes symptoms that *look* exactly like rabies. Roundworm is *not* airborne—it can only be transmitted through the oral-fecal route—the ingestion of an infected animal's feces.

Q: I set a trap for a woodchuck and caught a skunk. Help!

A: This is a common occurrence when traps are left open at night. You can let the skunk out without getting sprayed just by knowing that skunks have terrible eyesight and spray only when something comes at them fast, like a dog. If you move

---

*Contains animal-based ingredients.

slowly and talk soothingly, you shouldn't get sprayed. Skunks stamp their front feet as a warning when they're nervous, so if the skunk stamps, just remain motionless for a minute until he stops stamping, then proceed. You can drape a towel—slowly—over the trap prior to opening it. Once the trap door is opened, the skunk will beeline for home! If you must trap and relocate a woodchuck, remember to close the trap at night so another skunk doesn't get caught.

Q: Why not just trap the woodchuck family?

A: Trapping won't solve the problem. As long as woodchuck habitat is available, there will be woodchucks. Even in studies where all the woodchucks are trapped out of an area, others from the surrounding area quickly move into the vacated niche. In addition, trapping and relocating woodchucks may lead to starving young being left be-hind. Homeowners are then horrified to smell a foul odor. It's much more effective to simply exclude woodchucks from areas where they're not wanted.

We discourage trapping unless an animal is stuck somewhere and can't get out, or poses an immediate threat to humans or domestic animals. If you do hire a nuisance trapper, be sure to read our "Standards for Working with a Nuisance Wildlife Control Operator" brochure first to ensure that humane practices are followed and no animals are orphaned in the process.

Written by Laura Simon
Urban Wildlife Director

The Fund for Animals • 200 W. 57th St., New York, NY 10019 • (212) 246-2096 • FAX: (212) 246-2633 • www.fund.org

Common Misconceptions about Rabies

Often people are in a panic about rabies due to misleading media articles and folklore. It is vital to understand the facts about rabies, correct exaggerated fears, and know what sensible precautions you can take to prevent rabies exposure, such as vaccinating your companion animals and getting prompt post-exposure shots if bitten by a possibly rabid animal. Given all the media attention, people are surprised to learn that very few people die from rabies nationwide each year. Human fatalities due to lightning strikes and bad hamburgers far exceed the number of human deaths due to rabies. This doesn't mean we shouldn't be concerned about rabies; it means we should take sensible precautions, use common sense, and calm down!

General Concerns

Q: *Can't I get rabies by sitting on the grass a rabid animal drooled on last night?*

A: The virus cannot penetrate intact skin. *People can only get rabies via a bite from a rabid animal or through scratches, abrasions, open wounds, or mucous membranes contaminated with saliva or brain tissue from a rabid animal.** In addition, the virus is short-lived when exposed to the open air—the virus isn't viable after saliva dries up. If you are handling a companion animal who has been in a fight with a potentially rabid animal, take precautions such as using gloves to prevent contact with any still-fresh saliva.

Q: *Can rabies be spread through feces or blood?*

A: Rabies is *not* transmitted through the blood, urine, or feces of an infected animal, nor is it spread airborne through the open environment. *Saliva* provides the primary transmission medium when the animal is in the clinical stage of rabies. For the rabies virus to get to the salivary glands, it has to travel first from the site of entry (usually a bite wound) *through* the animal's nervous system, then to the brain. This is what causes most rabid animals to exhibit abnormal behaviors, depending on what part of the brain is infected. Finally, the virus travels to the salivary glands during the terminal stage of rabies, prior to death. It is this latter

stage of rabies when an animal is most infectious because the virus is in the saliva.

Q: *Don't many people die every year of rabies in the U.S.?*

A: Luckily, *no human has ever died from the raccoon strain of rabies*, according to the Centers for Disease Control and Prevention (CDC). The handful of human deaths from rabies annually (average 2.4 a year, nationwide) has been largely due to a *domestic bat strain* or *canine strain from abroad*. Between 1981 and 2000, there were a total of 42 human fatalities to rabies, of which 62 percent were *bat strain* (primarily silver-haired variant) and 31 percent were *canine strain* contracted overseas or in Mexico. No human fatalities to rabies were reported nationally in 1999. This low incidence doesn't mean we can't contract rabies; it just means we should continue taking sensible precautions to prevent exposures and seek prompt post-exposure prophylaxis when advised to do so by a doctor or local health department.

Species-Specific Concerns

BATS

Q: *Don't a lot of bats carry rabies?*

A: Actually, a very small percentage of bats carry rabies, much less than 1 percent of the population. However, if you suspect that a rabid bat has bitten you, or if a bat is found in the room where a person is sleeping, current health guidelines require that the bat be tested for rabies. Contact your local health department for instructions.

Q: *Help! I need to get a bat out of my house!*

A: Often healthy bats fly into houses through open windows or flues. In late summer, fledgling bats leave the roost for the first time and often take a wrong turn and end up inside a house. If there has been *no exposure,** the best way to evict the bat is to open all windows and doors and give the bat a

---

*If people are unsure about whether or not they have broken skin on their hands, suggest that they put their hands in rubbing alcohol to see if and where it stings.

*Exposure is defined as either bite exposure: any penetration of the skin by the teeth of a rabid animal, or nonbite exposure: scratches, abrasions, open wounds, or mucous membranes contaminated with saliva or brain tissue from a rabid animal. Nonbite exposures from terrestrial animals rarely cause rabies. (Source: *Advisory Committee on Immunization Practices*)

chance to fly out. A bat can be safely captured by putting a coffee can or shoebox over the bat and sliding a piece of cardboard underneath (unlike birds, bats cannot fly from the ground *up*, so be sure to put the bat on a tree limb or wall, off the ground). Often bats roost in attics and raise their young there, which provides a benefit to the homeowner in terms of mosquito control in the summer. The best eviction method is to create a one-way door over the attic's entry hole so that the bats can get out but not back in (see www.batcon.org for more information). *Warning:* Baby bats are too young to fly from May to August; therefore, any eviction should take place in the fall or very early spring to prevent orphaning.

Q: Don't bats fly into people's hair?

A: Contrary to popular belief, bats do not fly into people's hair. Their swooping flight pattern is due to their long wingspan and their need to gain momentum when flying in an enclosed space like a room. They will gain altitude near the walls and lose altitude near the center of the room, giving bystanders the *feeling* that they are being attacked when actually the bat is just trying to stay airborne!

FOXES

Q: There is a fox running around in the day, so the animal must be rabid.

A: Foxes haven't read the textbooks telling them to be nocturnal. It is quite common to see foxes hunting by day. It is normal too for the kits to be seen playing by themselves, seeming to have no parents around, and perhaps showing little fear of people. There's usually no need for intervention—soon the parents will appear and soon the kits will learn to be wary of humans. You can bang aluminum pot lids together to help teach the foxes to be fearful of people. Only if the kits look weak or sickly should your local fish and game agency be called to help you locate a wildlife rehabilitator.

RACCOONS

Q: I see a baby raccoon outside in the day—does that mean the animal is rabid?

A: When baby raccoons are orphaned, they don't know night from day—they only know that they are extremely hungry. This is when they tend to plunge out of trees. If the mother raccoon does not retrieve the baby after several hours (she rarely leaves her young alone for very long), then use

gloves, a shovel, or a trowel to put the baby in a cardboard box with a ventilated top (like a window screen) and an old shirt or cloth for comfort. The cub can be left out for a few hours after dusk to see if the mother retrieves him. Another option is to put an upside-down laundry basket over the cub with a weight on top so the cub doesn't wander off in the meantime. Be sure to put a cloth in for warmth and keep an eye on the weather. If the cub is not retrieved at night, it's a sure sign something has happened to the mother. Do not touch the raccoon with your bare hands. Call your local fish and game agency for the name of the nearest rehabilitator who is licensed to take in raccoons, as long as no exposure has occurred. If exposure has occurred, see "Exposure" section.

SKUNKS

Q: There's a baby skunk running around by day—is the skunk rabid?

A: It's possible, yet it's more likely that the skunk has lost sight of the mother because skunks are so near-sighted. If there's no risk of human contact, watch to see if the baby finds the den or if the mother retrieves him. Sometimes as baby skunks get older, they come out to explore while the mother is away. Most of the time they don't appear without her, however. An orphaned baby will appear frantic. If the skunk appears to be truly orphaned, call your local fish and game agency to locate a wildlife rehabilitator. Keep an eye on, but don't touch, the skunk and keep all people and companion animals away. You can put a plastic laundry basket upside down over the skunk to temporarily contain the animal while waiting for the mother to return. Approach the skunk slowly and talk softly—if the skunk gives a warning by stamping the front feet, then stand still or back off. You can approach again after the animal calms down. Do not risk being bitten.

OPOSSUMS

Q: There's an opossum hissing and drooling at me—is the opossum rabid?

A: For unknown reasons, opossums are amazingly resistant to rabies. Hissing, drooling, and swaying are part of the opossum's bluff routine to scare *you* off. Unlike other animals, opossums don't always flee when they're scared. Just leave the opossum alone and eventually the animal will wander off.

WOODCHUCKS

Q: I see a woodchuck circling and falling over—is it rabies?

A: For some unknown reason, woodchucks are the only rodents with a higher reporting rate for rabies in the eastern United States. Woodchucks are susceptible to the roundworm brain parasite, which causes signs that *look* exactly like rabies. Roundworm is transmitted through the ingestion of an infected animal's feces. Keep people and companion animals away from any sick-acting woodchuck and contact your local animal control officer or rehabilitator for assistance.

SQUIRRELS

Q: I see a squirrel circling and falling over—is it rabies?

A: Squirrels rarely get rabies. A more common, fatal problem for squirrels is the roundworm parasite that infects the brain and results in signs similar to rabies. Unfortunately, roundworm is usually fatal for squirrels. Another look-alike symptom in squirrels is head trauma, caused by being hit by a car. Contact your local wildlife rehabilitator or fish and game agency to assess strange squirrel behavior.

Exposure

If you have been bitten or scratched by a potentially rabid animal, wash the wound thoroughly with soap, monitor the biting animal's whereabouts, and contact your local health department for instructions and your local animal control officer for assistance in capturing the animal for rabies testing. If you have questions about rabies or other infectious diseases of public health importance, contact your state health department.

The Stats on Rabies

People often ask, "So how many humans have died of raccoon rabies?" The answer, to everyone's surprise, is "None." The Centers for Disease Control and Prevention has compiled statistics on the number and type of human rabies cases in the United States since 1980. Interestingly, most of the human rabies cases (two to three annually) have resulted from a canine strain contracted overseas or from the bat strain. Most of the bat cases have been of the silver-haired bat strain, which is surprising, since this species is rarely found in or around human houses.

Written by Laura Simon,
Urban Wildlife Director

The Fund for Animals • 200 West 57th St., New York, NY 10019 • (212) 246-2096 • FAX: (212) 246-2633 • www.fund.org

Solving Skunk Problems—The Sweetness of Skunks

Skunks are one of the most misunderstood wild animals. People don't realize that the skunk is a very docile, benign animal. However, their severe near-sightedness often gets them in trouble. Their odor is famous and strikes fear in everyone who encounters them. A skunk's only defense is a noxious odor created by a sulfuric acid "fired" from the anal glands. But skunks have a limited supply of ammunition and they can't "reload" very quickly, so they don't waste their defensive spray. Instead, they stamp their front feet as a warning if another creature gets too close, giving ample opportunity for the "threat" to back off. Skunks have a hearty appetite for grubs, frogs, insects, mice, and baby rats. People soon find that their rodent problems disappear after skunks take up residence.

SPRAYING REMEDIES

Q: I can smell skunk spray in my house—what should I do?

A: The nontoxic deodorizer Odors Away™ can be inexpensively purchased at hardware stores. It will instantly neutralize any bad odor indoors. Just put a few drops in a bowl, and place it in any room that smells. Add a few more drops every 24 hours.

Q: My dog has been sprayed. How do I remove the stench?

A: There are a number of widely publicized home remedies—such as tomato juice—which are ineffective at removing skunk odor. Wayward dogs can be instantly deodorized by a simple recipe.

MAGICAL SKUNK DEODORIZER RECIPE

For dogs, clothes, skin, etc.
* 1 quart 3% hydrogen peroxide
* 1/4 cup baking soda
* 1 teaspoon liquid dish or laundry soap

Mix these three ingredients together, then dip a wash rag in the solution and rub down the dog. Rinse and the odor will disappear within minutes! A word of warning: Hydrogen peroxide may give a dark-furred animal "rust-colored highlights."

SOLVING WILDLIFE CONFLICTS

Q: How do I get a skunk out of my garage?

A: Skunks commonly wander into garages when the door is left open. Open the garage door before dusk and sprinkle an 8-inch band of flour under it so you can watch for a track of exiting footprints. Close the door after you ensure the skunk is gone.

Q: There's a skunk in my window well; why doesn't he jump out?

A: Skunks are poor climbers. If the window well is shallow (under 2 feet), place a piece of wood at an angle less than 45 degrees to serve as a plank. For traction, tack a towel or chicken wire to the board. If the window well is deep, place smelly cheese or canned cat food in the far corner of an animal carrier (or plastic rectangular garbage can tipped on its side) and slowly lower it into the window well. The skunk, enticed by the food, will walk right in. Slowly raise the can or box to ground level, elevator-style, keeping your hands on the outside of the container so you don't risk being bitten. The skunk will soon amble out. Skunks have terrible eyesight and will *not* spray you if you move slowly and talk softly. Remember, skunks also give a warning by stamping their front feet, which gives you a chance to back off. It's vital to then purchase or make a window well cover (out of heavy mesh) or this situation will repeat itself.

Q: Skunks are digging up my lawn! How do I stop this?

A: This is a seasonal problem associated with periods of heavy rain or overwatering. The skunks are merely digging up grubs that come close to the surface of the soil when the ground is wet. As soon as the soil dries, the grubs will descend, the skunks won't smell them, and grubbing activity will cease. Although unsightly, this activity will not permanently damage the lawn. The easiest solution is merely to wait it out. Also, be careful not to overwater your lawn. To repel the skunks, sprinkle cayenne pepper on the lawn, or spray a homemade mix of 1 cup castor oil, 1 cup liquid dish soap, mixed with a gallon of water (in a spray can) to deter the skunks from grubbing in certain areas. A long-term solution is to purchase Milky Spore™, natural, nontoxic bacteria that will spread in the soil and kill the grubs, from a local garden store. However, the bacteria spread slowly and may take over a year to work. We do not recommend commercial diazinon-based products due to potential toxicity to children, companion animals, and the environment.

In addition, skunks are often wrongly blamed for eating garden vegetables. They are actually eating all the Japanese beetles, grubs, and other insect pests. To keep animals out of your garden, create an L-shaped barrier (see below).

Q: How do I get a skunk family out from under my deck/shed?

A: Skunks will take advantage of cavities under decks and sheds to raise their young. However, they are nomadic by nature and will usually leave when the young are old enough. The simplest option is to wait for the skunks to leave on their own, and then seal off their entry hole with hardware cloth. We don't recommend trapping because starving young are likely to be left behind. You can encourage the skunks to evict themselves sooner by spraying a repellent around your shed or poking some ammonia-sprinkled rags underneath, yet be careful not to poke the skunks!

Eviction: If you can't wait for the skunks to leave on their own:

1. Wait a few weeks until you see the babies come out with their mother (watch after dusk) and then seal their entry hole, as described below.

2. *Seal up the shed except for one main opening.* Place a pre-made one-way door (sold mail order by ACES, 800-338-ACES, or Tomahawk Live Trap Company, 800-272-8727) over that one remaining exit and leave it in place for three to seven days so all animals can get out but not back in. To ensure that all animals are out from under the deck before sealing it off permanently, put a layer of flour on the inside and outside of the door after installation, and leave it in place for one or two nights. Any footprints in the flour should be outside the door and none inside. *Do not try this technique until the young are mobile and start following the mother on outings. Otherwise young skunks will starve under the deck.*

3. If the problem occurs in late summer/fall, and you're sure there's only one animal underneath the deck, sprinkle white flour outside the hole and check after dark for exiting footprints. You can also put balled-up newspaper in the hole. If the newspaper hasn't moved for three to four days, the den has been vacated.

Repellents: The size of the denning space and the amount of ventilation will largely influence if a repellent will work. We recommend using ammonia-soaked rags, lights, and a blaring radio to convert an attractive space (quiet, dark, and protected) into one that is inhospitable. Here are some repellents that have proven effective at repelling skunks under certain circumstances:

1. A Castor Oil Formula
1 cup castor oil
1 cup liquid soap
mix these 2 ingredients together, then add: 1 gallon of water to a spray can. Spray around den area.

2. Hot Pepper repellent*
1 chopped yellow onion
1 chopped Jalapeno pepper
1 tablespoon cayenne pepper
Boil ingredients for 20 minutes in 2 quarts of water. Let it cool, and strain mixture through cheesecloth. Apply with spray bottle around the denning area. Don't spray too deeply into the hole or the skunk may reciprocate! It only lasts three to five days, so you will need to reapply if the animals' behavior is not modified. (*This information courtesy of Jack Murphy, Urban Wildlife Rescue, Inc.)

3. Cayenne pepper
Sprinkle around denning area.

Exclusion: *The necessary final step!* After completing one of the above steps, create an L-shaped barrier by covering the entry hole with hardware cloth and sinking it 4–6 inches into the ground. Then bend it at a 90-degree angle, away from the deck, for 8–12 inches to create a false bottom so the animals don't dig under the barrier. Check the next day for signs of digging from the inside to ensure that no skunk was sealed in.

Q: I have a cat door and found a skunk in my house. What do I do?

A: Try to isolate the skunk in one room by closing all doors and erecting barriers (such as screens or boards, which gently funnel the skunk back out the way he came in). Cat doors pose a continual problem because skunks and other wildlife smell the cat food inside and can't resist. We recommend eliminating cat doors altogether and training your cats to come for food at a certain time in the middle of the day, while nocturnal wild animals are sleeping! If you must have a cat door, either lock it at night (remember, skunks are generally nocturnal) or get the magnetic kind, which only opens when signaled by a collar on your cat's neck (available from RC Steele Company, 800-872-3773).

Q: There's a skunk in my pool. How do I get him out?

A: Skunks fall into pools fairly often because of their poor eyesight. You can easily save the skunk by putting a pool skimmer or broom underneath him. Often the skunks are exhausted from swimming and may need some time to recover. If the skunk does not leave on his own after two hours, contact your local state fish and game agency to locate a wildlife rehabilitator.

Q: I see a dead mother skunk by the side of the road surrounded by babies. What should I do?

A: Contact a licensed rehabilitator to help you. In the meantime, you can put an upside-down laundry basket over the skunks so they don't wander off, and alert the police to your efforts.

Q: There is a skunk with a yogurt cup stuck on his head. What do I do?

A: Unfortunately, certain yogurt cups have a very dangerous design—the top has a small opening and rim that entraps a skunk's torpedo-shaped head. Skunks caught in these cups soon become dehydrated and oxygen-deprived, and starve to death. The skunk won't spray anything he can't see, so hold the yogurt cup firmly, in a gloved hand. Upon feeling resistance, the skunk will pull back and his head should pop out. Stand motionless, and the skunk will not see or spray you. Another less "hands-on" option is to put a laundry basket or milk crate over the skunk (with a heavy rock on top) to keep him from wandering, and then contact a wildlife rehabilitator. (Likewise, skunks will accidentally lodge their heads in dumpster drain holes that aren't properly screened. Contact a rehabilitator for assistance in this circumstance.)

Q: I set a trap for a woodchuck and caught a skunk. How do I get him out without getting sprayed?

A: This is a common occurrence when traps are left out all night. You can get the skunk out without getting sprayed just by moving slowly and talking soothingly. Remain motionless for a minute if he starts stamping his front feet and raises his tail, and then proceed when the stamping stops. You can drape a towel—slowly—over the trap prior to opening it to create a visual barrier. Once the trap door is opened, the skunk will beeline for home. If you must trap and relocate a woodchuck, remember to close the trap at night so another skunk doesn't get trapped inadvertently.

DISEASE AND SAFETY CONCERNS

Q: Do skunks carry rabies?

A: Skunks may contract their own strain of rabies (in central U.S.) or serve as a "spill-over" species for other variants. Since 1980, only one

human death has been attributed to the skunk strain of rabies anywhere in the United States! According to the Centers for Disease Control and Prevention, the few human deaths to rabies (on average two to three a year, nationwide) have been largely due to domestic bat strains or canine strains contracted overseas. It's important to take proper precautions by calling your local animal control officer if you observe a sick, disoriented-acting skunk in areas where rabies occurs.

Q: There is a skunk in my yard during the daytime. Isn't the skunk rabid?

A. Even though skunks are nocturnal, they sometimes forage by day, particularly in the spring, when they have young and may be extra hungry. If an adult skunk seen in the daytime is also showing abnormal behavior, such as paralysis, circling, unprovoked aggression, screeching, self-mutilation, or uncharacteristic tameness, call your local animal control officer or police department for assistance and keep all companion animals and children away from the animal.

Q: There's a baby skunk running around by day. Is the baby rabid?

A: It's possible, yet it's more likely that the skunk has lost sight of the mother. Watch to see if the baby finds the den or if the mother retrieves him. You can put a plastic laundry basket upside down over the skunk to temporarily contain the animal while waiting for the mother to return. Approach the skunk slowly and talk softly—if the skunk gives a warning by stamping the front feet, then stand still or back off. You can approach again after the animal calms down. As baby skunks get older, they sometimes come out to explore while the mother is away. Most of the time they don't appear without her, however. An orphaned baby will be frantic. If the skunk appears to be truly orphaned, call your local fish and game agency to locate a wildlife rehabilitator. Keep an eye on the skunk and keep all people and companion animals away.

Q: Do I have to worry about my children being attacked by a skunk?

A: Skunks are not aggressive. Again, their defense is spraying rather than biting or scratching. Due to their near-sightedness, skunks may wander up to a child, or orphaned young may follow a child, unable to discern that it's a person. These instances are infrequent, yet it is vital to teach your child to avoid any contact with wild animals and instead enjoy watching them from afar.

TRAPPING: IS IT NECESSARY?

Q: Do I need to pay a nuisance control trapper to solve my problem?

A: Although people's gut reaction may be to "get rid of the skunks," trapping will not solve the problem because skunks from the surrounding area will soon replace any removed. As long as there's skunk habitat, there will be skunks. Trapping merely creates turnover in the population.

In addition, nuisance wildlife control companies charge a fee—sometimes hundreds of dollars—for problems that homeowners often can resolve themselves. And when animals are trapped during the birthing season, starving babies may be left behind. We discourage trapping unless an animal is stuck somewhere and can't get out, or poses an immediate threat to humans or domestic pets.

The answer is prevention through exclusion: animal-proof your home by sealing up all holes. For more information, contact The Fund for Animals' Wildlife Hotline at 203-389-4411.

Written by Laura Simon,
Urban Wildlife Director

The Fund for Animals • 200 W. 57th St., New York, NY 10019 • (212) 246-2096 • FAX: (212) 246-2633 • www.fund.org

Living with Squirrels

NATURAL HISTORY

Squirrels are highly intelligent, inquisitive, and skillful creatures—all characteristics that often lead people to rank squirrels number one on the list of troublemakers. Squirrels eat nuts and large seeds during the fall and winter; fruits, berries, mushrooms, and insects during the summer; and bird seed any time of the year! Squirrels are diurnal animals, meaning they are active during the day. Squirrels are seldom far from trees; they rely on trees for shelter, to escape from predators, and to bear and raise their young. However, as people continue to cut down more and more trees, squirrels have adapted by utilizing almost anything that looks or acts like a tree for their activities. As a result, squirrels often make their way into attics, chimneys, and crawl spaces along upper levels of houses. Fortunately, there are ways to live peacefully with the squirrels in your environment.

Q: How do I keep squirrels out of my bird feeder?

A: The best thing to do to prevent squirrels from eating out of your bird feeder is to keep them away from the beginning—once they become accustomed to food, they will be persistent at getting to it! There are a number of specialized feeders and baffles available that are considered "squirrel-proof." One effective squirrel baffle is shaped like a stovepipe and is placed on the pole portion of the bird feeder. This allows the squirrel to climb up the pole and into the closed pipe, but he can go no further. The pipe must be at least 15 inches long to prevent the squirrel from climbing over it, and set at least 4 feet off the ground (to the bottom part of the baffle) to prevent the squirrel from jumping over it. The feeder itself must be placed far enough away from nearby trees, wires, buildings, or any other objects a squirrel could use to jump on top of the feeder. You may also want to try stocking your feeder with seeds that are undesirable to squirrels, such as safflower seeds, but attract birds such as cardinals and grosbeaks, or niger thistle, which will attract goldfinches and other songbirds. Another newly designed battery-operated bird feeder has a ledge that twirls when a squirrel lands on it, literally flipping the animal off. We strongly discourage the use of any capsaicin-based "hot pepper" powder mix, which, although advertised as a "humane" repellent when mixed with bird seed, reportedly can make squirrels sick and may be irritating to the humans that handle it.

Q: How do I get squirrels out of the attic?

A: Again, the best way to prevent squirrels from nesting in your attic is to keep them away from the beginning. Continued maintenance on your house is essential; prevent wildlife problems from occurring by sealing up all possible entry holes, trimming all overhanging tree branches, and installing a chimney cap.

Squirrels have two litters a year, one in early spring (February–May) and one in late summer (August–October). If you have a squirrel in your attic for more than a few days at those times of the year, the animal is most likely a mother with her babies. The best thing to do is wait six to eight weeks until the young are old enough to follow their mother on outings. Once the young are old enough to accompany her, and you observe this occurring, you can install a one-way door (available from Tomahawk Live Trap, 800-272-8727, or ACES, 800-338-ACES) over the entry hole, which will allow the squirrels to go out but not come back in.

If you absolutely *must* evict the squirrels before the young are old enough to leave on their own, you can place rags sprinkled with a strong-smelling household cleaner, like ammonia, along with a blaring radio tuned to an all-night rap or rock station, in the attic. Be careful not to place the ammonia rags too close to the nesting site, as the babies can be asphyxiated by the fumes. Also, illuminate the nest by shining lights on it. (You can generally locate the attic nest by looking near the entry hole for lumped-up insulation along the perimeter of the attic interior.) This will turn the squirrels' safe, quiet nesting environment into one that is smelly and frightening. If the mother knows of an alternate nesting site, she will often move her young that day. If she has to find or build a new nest, it may take longer.

Once you have not heard any sounds coming from the attic for several days, you need to make sure the squirrels have left before you seal the entrance hole. Place a soft plug, such as a paper towel or crumpled newspaper, in the entry hole and check the next day to see if it has been pushed out. Once you are completely sure the squirrels have abandoned their nest, you may remove the one-way door and patch the hole using 1/4-inch or 1/2-inch hardware cloth. Extend the hardware cloth 8–12 inches beyond the hole on all sides, and secure it over the hole using a staple gun and U-shaped nails. Next, spray the area with Ropel (found at some garden stores, can be ordered online from Burlington Scientific Corporation at www.gardeningdepot.com, or call 631-694-4700 to find a local distributor) or Miller's Hot Sauce (call 800-233-2040 to find a local distributor) to prevent any chewing. To make sure that no squirrels were inadvertently trapped in the attic, put flour down in front of the entry hole and check the next day for footprints of any squirrel left behind. Continue to listen for sounds of activity in the attic, and watch to see if a squirrel is persistent in attempts to gain entry from the outside—a mother squirrel will go to great lengths to reunite with her young, and can cause extensive damage in the process.

If you notice squirrel activity in your attic during the winter months and you are positive there are no babies present, you may use the one-way door or exclusion methods as described above. Exclude the squirrels at mid-morning on a warm, sunny day when the squirrels are out eating. Again, listen for any squirrels inadvertently trapped inside the attic. However, remember that if you evict a squirrel from your attic during the winter, the squirrel may not find, or be able to create, a vacant cavity and may freeze to death. For this reason, consider waiting until early spring to do an eviction.

Relocating a squirrel by trapping may sound kind, but it is usually a death sentence for the squirrel. In the winter, squirrels bury a food cache that supports them. If relocated at this time of year, they will most likely die. Trapping and relocating squirrels at other times of the year subjects them to being run out by other territorial squirrels, being preyed upon, and being hit by cars as they frantically search for the habitat they know.

Q: There's a squirrel loose in the house—how do I get him out?

A: Squirrels enter houses by accident, and often frantically search for a way out. Create a clear-cut path to the outdoors for the squirrel by closing all doors to any rooms in the house that the squirrel is not in, and darkening all windows and doors except for the one you want him to go out. Make sure that there is a chair or piece of furniture that the squirrel can use to reach a windowsill, if necessary.

If the squirrel is in a ground-level room, he should head toward daylight and will find his way out if left alone. If the squirrel is trapped in a second-story location, hang a knotted bedsheet out of the window to provide the squirrel with something to climb down upon.

If you are unable to create an exit, set a live trap* on the floor near the squirrel, baited with peanut butter, and leave him alone for a few hours. Once the squirrel is trapped and released outside of the house, it is important to look around for any possible ways he might have entered. Carefully and thoroughly inspect the inside and outside of your house for possible entry points. Check for tracks of soot around the fireplace or dust around the furnace. Also check your attic (on a sunny day) for an entrance hole that may need patching.

Q: How do I get a squirrel out of my chimney? My fireplace?

A: *Under absolutely no circumstances should you try to smoke an animal out of your chimney—you will succeed only in burning or killing the animal!*

Once again, prevention is the key. It is absolutely essential to have a chimney cap installed by a chimney sweep to prevent any animals from falling down, or nesting in, your chimney.

If you hear a squirrel scrambling around in your chimney, it is safe to assume that he is stuck unless you have seen evidence that he can climb out. To provide the squirrel with a means for escape, lower a thick (3/4-inch) rope down the chimney, making sure it is long enough to reach the damper. Tie one end of the rope to the top of the chimney to secure it in place, and the squirrel should climb up on his own within daylight hours. If a rope is not available, you can tie knotted bedsheets together to create a makeshift rope.

If the squirrel is in your fireplace, the best thing to do is place a live trap baited with peanut butter in the fireplace behind the fireplace doors. Typically the squirrel will huddle in the back corner of the fireplace when the doors are opened, and will stay there as you place the trap slowly and quietly just inside the doors. Close the doors to the fireplace and leave the room to wait for the squirrel to enter the trap, then simply release him outside.

Note: As a precaution, you may want to prepare a "funnel" system leading out an open door before attempting to place the live trap inside the fire-

---

*You can usually get a live trap from your animal control facility, a Rent-It store, or a hardware store.

place. While most squirrels will huddle in the far corner of the fireplace when the doors are opened, they may also bolt into the room out of fear. Tables and chairs tipped on their side can create a path out an open door.

Finally, be sure to have a proper chimney cap installed by a chimney sweep once the squirrel is captured and released outside so this problem does not happen again. Also, to prevent squirrels from getting onto your roof, trim any overhanging tree branches and block access from the trunks of trees adjacent to your house.

Q: How do I prevent squirrels from climbing up a tree into my attic or chimney?

A: First and foremost, it is important to make sure there are no active nests in the tree. Then, take a 3-foot-wide section of sheet metal and drill a hole in each of the four corners. Next, wrap the sheet metal around the tree, but instead of harming the tree by hammering the metal into place with nails, secure the two ends together using two metal coils running between the drilled holes. This way the protective band will stretch as the tree grows. The sheet-metal band must be at least 4 feet above ground level and at least 3 feet wide to prevent squirrels from climbing up the tree and jumping over it.

Q: A squirrel is looking disoriented and falling over. Is he rabid?

A: Like all warm-blooded mammals, squirrels are susceptible to the rabies virus. However, the incidence of rabies in squirrels is extremely low, and squirrel-to-human transmission of the virus has not been documented. This stems in part from the fact that squirrels are such small animals. If a squirrel were to tangle with a rabid animal, most often he would not survive the attack long enough to incubate and transmit the virus by biting another animal. The squirrel may be looking disoriented for a number of reasons: he may have been hit by a car; fallen from a tree; or be suffering from roundworm, a parasite that affects the brain. The symptoms of all three look similar to rabies. Roundworm is *not* airborne—it can only be transmitted through the oral-fecal route—the ingestion of an infected animal's feces.

To help this squirrel, contact your state fish and game agency or humane society for assistance and a possible referral. However, roundworm is a fatal illness and you must carefully evaluate whether or not the trauma of a trip to a veterinarian or reha-bilitator is more humane than simply allowing the squirrel to die a natural death.

Q: How do I keep squirrels from eating my garden tomatoes?

A: Squirrels not only help themselves to your prize-winning tomatoes, but they have the audacity to take just one bite and discard the rest! However, this is usually because squirrels are not particularly fond of tomatoes or other vegetables, but will eat them if hungry enough. So, the first thing to do is to make sure that squirrels are actually the nibblers! (A more likely scenario is that you have a woodchuck dining on your tomatoes.)

If there is a squirrel eating the tomatoes, rest assured that this is a temporary inconvenience and will subside shortly. To protect your tomatoes in the meantime, you can use a repellent called Hinder (available through your local garden store or Forest & Wildlife, 800-647-5368), which is safe for human consumption.

Q: How can I stop squirrels from digging holes in my yard?

A: The good news is that this digging is a seasonal phenomenon, and rarely causes significant damage to lawns. Squirrels bury nuts in the ground for later retrieval during the winter and early spring months. Interestingly, the squirrels that bury the nuts are not always the ones that dig them up, since squirrels retrieve nuts using their keen sense of smell—not memory! The easiest solution is to wait a few weeks and let the problem end on its own. However, if you absolutely must prevent squirrels from digging in your yard, you can sprinkle some cayenne pepper on the affected areas.

Q: How do I stop squirrels from chewing holes in the wood trim or stucco on my house?

A: Sometimes squirrels will chew the trim on a house for unknown reasons, particularly in winter. The cause may be a mineral deficiency, but no one knows for sure. The solution is to spray Ropel (found at some garden stores, can be ordered online from Burlington Scientific Corporation at www.gardeningdepot.com, or call 631-694-4700 to find a local distributor) or Miller's Hot Sauce (call 800-233-2040 to find a local distributor) on the affected areas to prevent any chewing. It is a good idea to pretest the repellent on a small section of the trim or stucco first if you are at all unsure of the paint used on your house. Some repellents can cause discoloration of latex paint if the paint has been mixed with certain ingredients.

Q: I cut down a dead tree and found a nest of baby squirrels! What should I do?

A: Give the mother a chance to reclaim her young. If the babies fell from the tree uninjured, leave them where they are, leave the area, and keep people and companion animals away. Monitor from a safe distance; if the babies are not retrieved by nighttime, contact your state fish and game agency or local humane society to locate a licensed wildlife rehabilitator near you. If there is any risk of predation, you can put the squirrels in a wicker basket and attach the basket securely to the tree. Do not cover the squirrels with leaves or blankets because the mother may not be able to find them. If it is chilly outside, provide the babies with a heat source, such as a portable heating pad, a hot water bottle, or rig up a heating pad using an extension cord.

Q: Why not just trap and relocate the squirrels in my yard?

A: Squirrels are territorial animals, so your resident squirrels are actually keeping other squirrels away from your yard. If you remove the existing squirrels, others will quickly move in and your problems will continue. Also, trapping and relocating squirrels often leads to starving young being left behind. Homeowners are then horrified to smell a foul odor. The only permanent solution is to eliminate the problematic behavior, rather than the animal, using the strategies described here.

We discourage trapping unless an animal is stuck somewhere and can't get out, or poses an immediate threat to humans or domestic animals. If you do hire a nuisance trapper, we recommend that you find someone who will give you a written guarantee that he will (1) use nonlethal methods only, (2) release the animals together (so juveniles aren't separated from their mothers) and release them on-site (relocated animals have low survival rates when released in unfamiliar areas), and (3) do the necessary exclusion and repair work to prevent wild animals from entering your home. Ask the right questions so you don't pay hundreds of dollars for an inhumane "solution."

A NOTE ABOUT FLYING SQUIRRELS

Flying squirrels are small squirrels (approximately 9 inches from nose to tail tip) that people rarely get the chance to see. They have bulgy, shiny black eyes, a flat tail, and a loose skin flap that extends from the foreleg to the hind leg. This flap allows the squirrels to glide through the air, or "fly." Flying squirrels most often nest in abandoned woodpecker holes or natural tree cavities, in birdhouses, and sometimes even in attics.

Unlike gray squirrels, flying squirrels are nocturnal and highly sociable animals. Therefore, if you are hearing squirrel activity in your attic at night, you may have flying squirrels—and you may have a colony! The methods for evicting flying squirrels are similar to the ones used for gray squirrels. If you absolutely *must* evict the squirrels before the young are old enough to leave on their own, simply place rags sprinkled with ammonia, along with a blaring radio tuned to a rap or rock station, in the attic. This will turn the squirrels' safe and quiet environment into one that is smelly and frightening.

Since flying squirrels are active at night, it is difficult to determine when the young are old enough to start following their mother on nightly outings. For this reason, one-way doors (available from Tomahawk Live Trap, 800-272-8727, or ACES, 800-338-ACES) should be a last resort and used only during midsummer or late fall, and avoided at all other times.

Live traps should also be avoided, as flying squirrels tend to become highly stressed and have a high mortality rate when trapped. Many state fish and game agencies actually require that you get a special permit and approval to trap flying squirrels. Under no circumstances should glue traps be used to capture any wild animal, including flying squirrels. They are inefficient and extremely inhumane.

Written by Becca deWeerdt
Urban Wildlife Program

The Fund for Animals • 200 W. 57th St., New York, NY 10019 • (888) 405-FUND • FAX: (212) 246-2633 • www.fund.org

Glossary

algae—tiny floating plants that grow in water. High concentrations of blooming algae in the ocean cause a condition known as red tide.

aviary—a large enclosure for birds. A bird being rehabilitated is moved to an aviary when it's well enough to fly.

beached—to be stuck in sand or shallow water onshore. Humphrey, a humpback whale, beached in a river of shallow water.

biology—the study of all life-forms.

birds of prey (also known as raptors)—birds that hunt other animals for food. Birds of prey use sharp talons to capture and kill prey and hooked beaks to tear the meat.

blind—a hiding place for observing or hunting wildlife. One rehabilitator used her car as a blind when watching a barn owl nest.

blowhole—a nostril (or two) in the top of whales' or dolphins' heads. When a dolphin surfaces, it exhales, spraying water through its blowhole, before it inhales.

blubber—fat. Most marine mammals have a lot of blubber to protect them from cold water.

buoyant—able to float. Because whales are buoyant, their massive weight is held up by the water.

captive breeding—the breeding of wild animals in captivity. Captive breeding has helped increase the numbers of black-footed ferrets, which are among the most endangered mammals on earth.

carrion—dead animals. Vultures do us a favor by eating carrion, especially alongside roads.

cetaceans—marine mammals that include whales, dolphins, and porpoises. Cetaceans are very intelligent animals with strong family bonds.

conscious breathing—nonautomatic breathing that requires part of the brain to stay awake. Because of conscious breathing, cetaceans never sleep deeply.

crepuscular—active mostly at dawn and dusk. Deer and rabbits are crepuscular creatures.

dehydration—loss of body fluids. Dehydration is a problem with many sick animals because they're too sick to eat or drink.

den—to sleep for the winter. Bears den in logs or caves.

dental acrylic—substance used by dentists on human teeth because it hardens when mixed correctly. Sometimes dental acrylic is used to repair cracked turtle shells.

diurnal—active during the daytime. With the exception of owls, birds of prey are diurnal hunters.

domesticate—to tame wild animals. It took tens of thousands of years to domesticate wolves into the dogs we know today.

down—fuzzy, fluffy feathers. Nestling birds may be naked or covered with down.

ecology—the study of the relationship among plants, animals, and their habitats.

endangered species—animal species in danger of becoming extinct. Because there are only about 2,000 manatees left in the wild, they are considered endangered.

extinction—death of all the animals in a species, which will never exist again. The extinction of any species is a loss to all life.

euthanasia—the humane killing of sick or injured animals as an act of mercy or compassion. Euthanasia is a necessary part of wildlife rehabilitation.

fledgling—a young bird learning to fly. Fledglings are sometimes called "branchers" because they perch on branches near their nest.

flight cage—an enclosure large enough for birds to practice flying. Birds of Prey Foundation in Broomfield, Colorado, has some of the largest flight cages in the United States.

flyways—frequently traveled paths of migrating birds. The Pacific, Central, Mississippi, and Atlantic are the main flyways in the United States.

foot—to stab with talons. When rescuing raptors, you need to be careful to hold the birds' feet, or they may foot you.

forage—to search for food. Wild animal parents teach their young where to forage for foods.

formula—a substitute milk mixture for baby animals. Different species of animals require different formulas.

foster parents—animals usually of the same species that take care of orphaned babies. Male and female animals can make good foster parents.

freeze brand—a painless mark made on marine animals for identification. Previously rehabilitated dolphins in the wild are identified by freeze brands.

gaping—opening the mouth for food. Gaping baby birds get fed by their parents.

groom—to clean feathers or fur. Animals groom themselves to keep their fur waterproof and to keep their feathers waterproof and working perfectly for flight.

habitat—place where animals live naturally. A habitat provides food, water, space, and shelter.

haul-out areas—places where marine animals can climb out of the water. Floating docks at Pier 39 in San Francisco's Fisherman's Wharf are haul-out areas for sea lions.

herpetology—the study of reptiles and amphibians. Some rehabilitators study herpetology so they can treat snakes, frogs, and lizards.

hypothermia—low body temperature. Without blubber or fur, marine mammals would develop hypothermia from cold seawater.

imprint—when baby animals identify with their mothers and believe they are the same species. Baby geese imprint on the first creature they see.

incubator—an enclosure for baby animals with controlled heat and humidity. Naked nestling birds have to stay in incubators for warmth.

instinct—an animal's automatic response to something in its environment. A mother bear's instinct is to fight to protect her young.

jesses—short leather straps around the legs of raptors used for catching the birds and attaching leashes. Education raptors wear jesses in the classroom so they can be kept on a glove or stand.

locks—enclosures (as in canals) with gates at each end, used to raise boats as they pass from level to level. Some manatees are crushed when passing through locks.

maggots—fly larvae (grubs). Sometimes rehabilitators have to pick maggots out of animals' wounds.

mange—skin disease with itching and loss of hair, caused by a tiny parasite. Foxes can spread mange to people's pets and to people.

manning—training. Manning raptors to become education birds takes a lot of time and patience.

marine—pertaining to the sea. Most marine mammals spend all their time in the sea.

marsupial—an order of mammals in which females carry their young in a pouch. Opossums are the only marsupials native to North America.

mealworms—beetle larvae, used to feed insect-eating birds and mammals. Mealworms often are raised in rehabilitation centers and used for wildlife food.

migrate—to travel seasonally from one territory to another for feeding and breeding. Many U.S. birds migrate to Central and South America for the winter.

mites—tiny parasites that burrow under an animal's skin, causing itching, hair loss, and sometimes death. If infected with mites, animals can spread them, even in people's homes.

molt—to shed fur or feathers.

native—living or growing naturally in a place. Native animals often have no defenses against introduced animals such as cats and rats.

natural history—the habits, biology, and needs of wildlife. Knowing the natural history of wildlife is very important when caring for animals.

necropsy—medical examination of a dead animal. Necropsies were done on dead manatees to help scientists figure out what caused the massive die-off in 1996.

nestling—a young bird still in the nest. A nestling may be naked or it may have some feathers, but it can't fly.

nocturnal—active at night. Owls are nocturnal birds.

ornithology—the study of birds. Some rehabilitators are very knowledgeable about ornithology.

owl pellets—the undigestible parts of prey that owls spit up. If you look beneath trees where owls roost, you'll probably find owl pellets.

parasite—an organism that lives in or on another organism. Wild animals often have parasites, such as intestinal worms, and some can be passed to pets or people.

pinky—a hairless, pink, deaf, and blind newborn mammal. A pinky will die quickly without warmth.

poach—to hunt or trap illegally. We should all report people who poach wildlife.

postrelease study—research done on wildlife after release from rehabilitation centers, to check how they are doing. Postrelease studies on rehabilitated black bear cubs show that they tend to stay far away from people.

preen—to comb or clean feathers with a beak or bill. Birds preen frequently to keep their feathers clean and straight.

quarantine—isolation from other creatures for a period of time. Newly admitted animals are often put in quarantine to protect the other animals.

rabies—a viral disease transmitted by bites, scratches, or saliva from an infected animal. Without treatment, rabies is fatal.

rabies vector species—animals that most commonly carry and spread rabies. Rabies vector species usually include skunks, raccoons, bats, foxes, and coyotes.

raptor—bird of prey. Raptors are fascinating birds that help people by eating many rodents and insects.

red tide—discolored seawater caused by blooming algae. Red tide in high concentrations is toxic to fish and many marine animals.

regenerate—to grow back or heal. The injured tissue in a cracked turtle shell will regenerate in time if the turtle gets good medical treatment.

regurgitate—to throw up partially digested food. Some bird parents regurgitate food to feed their babies.

roost—to rest or sleep. Birds often roost in trees.

socialized—to be used to a person or another animal. If handled too much, wild animals can become socialized to humans, losing their protective fear.

strand—when marine animals go ashore or stay in shallow water where they wouldn't normally be, and they seem in distress. Usually, marine animals are sick or injured when they strand.

subcutaneous—delivered under the skin. Wildlife may receive subcutaneous fluids if they can't eat or drink.

surrogate—a substitute. Sometimes, rehabilitators use puppets or stuffed animals as surrogate mothers for orphaned animals.

talons—sharp, curved claws. Raptors use their talons to catch prey.

threatened species—species whose numbers have decreased dangerously but are not considered endangered. Brown pelicans are a threatened species.

tote—an enclosure with water. A rehabilitating otter swims in a portable tote.

tube-feed—to pass a narrow tube from an animal's mouth into its stomach in order to give it food, fluids, or medications. Rehabilitators sometimes tube-feed baby opossums.

ventilator—a machine that breathes for patients during surgery. Whales need to be on ventilators if they receive anesthesia.

veterinary technician—a licensed professional who is a veterinary assistant, much like an animal care nurse. Some wildlife rehabilitators are veterinary technicians.

vixen—a female fox. A vixen teaches her young how to hunt and avoid humans.

weaned—not nursing anymore. A young animal needs to find its own food if it's weaned.

wildlife rehabilitators—people who take care of orphaned, sick, or injured wildlife, with the purpose of restoring them to health and returning them to the wild. Wildlife rehabilitators have a lot of knowledge about wildlife injuries, diseases, and treatments.

zoology—the study of the biology of animals. Many rehabilitators study zoology to learn as much as possible about wildlife.

zoonoses—diseases passed from wildlife to people. Some zoonoses can be very dangerous, even fatal, for humans.

Resources

More and more books, videos, and websites about wildlife rehabilitation are created every year, and some are great resources. A few, however, do not present accurate or safe information about what to do when finding orphaned or hurt wildlife. For that reason, they were not included in the lists below.

Books on Wildlife Rescue and Rehabilitation

Picture Books

Cox, Lena Taylor. *Buddy the Eagle Who Thought He Was a People* (coloring book). Alaska Raptor Center, Sitka, AK (1-800-643-9425).

Dewey, Jennifer Owings. *Wildlife Rescue: The Work of Dr. Kathleen Ramsay.* Boyd Mills Press, 1994.

Farentinos, Robert C. *Winter's Orphans.* Roberts Rinehart Publishers, 1993.

Johnson, Sylvia. *Raptor Rescue.* Dutton Children's Books, 1995.

Kincheloe, Sandy. *When Birds Get Hurt* (coloring book). Alaska Raptor Center, Sitka, AK (1-800-643-9425).

Knapp, Toni. *The Six Bridges of Humphrey the Whale.* The Rockrimmon Press, Inc., 1989.

Martin, Jacqueline Briggs. *Washing the Willow Tree Loon.* Simon and Schuster Books for Young Readers, 1995.

McFarland, Sheryl. *Eagle Dreams.* Philomel Books, 1994.

Oldham, Pat, and Wildlife Rescue, Inc., of New Mexico. *Wildlife Rehabilitation: A Coloring and Activity Book.* Horizon Communications, 1995.

Scott, Jack Denton. *Orphans from the Sea.* Putnam, 1982.

Shachtman, Tom. *The Birdman of St. Petersburg.* Macmillan Publishing Co., 1982.

Tokuda, Wendy. *Humphrey the Lost Whale.* Heian International, Inc., 1986.

Other Books

Anderson, Laurie Halse. *Manatee Blues.* Wild at Heart Series. American Girl, Pleasant Company Publications, 2000.

———. *Trapped.* Wild at Heart Series. American Girl, Pleasant Company Publications, 2001.

The California Center for Wildlife. *Living with Wildlife.* Sierra Club Books, 1994.

Chubb, Kit. *The Avian Ark.* Hungry Mind Press, 1991.

Collett, Rosemary. *My Orphans of the Wild.* J. B. Lippincott Company, 1974.

Curtis, Patricia. *All Wild Creatures Welcome.* E. P. Dutton, 1985.

Ford, Barbara, and Stephen Ross. *Wildlife Rescue.* Albert Whiteman and Company, 1987.

The Humane Society of the United States. *Wild Neighbors: The Humane Approach to Living with Wildlife.* Fulcrum Publishing, 1997.

Jordan, W. J., and John Hughes. *Care of the Wild.* Rawson Associates, 1983.

Lollar, Amanda. *The Bat in My Pocket.* Capra Press, 1995.

McKeever, Katherine. *A Place for Owls.* Firefly Books, 1992.

McKenna, Virginia. *Into the Blue.* HarperSanFrancisco, 1992.

Stretch, Mary Jane, and Phyllis Hobe. *For the Love of Wild Things.* Stackpole Books, 1995.

Whitehead, Lynn, and Mark Steilen. *Sully the Seal and Alley the Cat.* Storytellers Ink, 1994.

Videos on Wildlife Rescue and Rehabilitation

Fly Away Home, movie and video, 1996.

Free Willy, movie and video, 1993.

Free Willy 2, movie and video, 1995.

You can rent the videos listed above from video stores with a good selection.

A Home for Pearl, four-part video (seventy minutes) and Instructional Guide for elementary school children, teaches about wildlife habitat, what wildlife need to survive, the difference between wild and domestic animals, predators, endangered species, and the effects of habitat loss. National Fish and Wildlife Foundation, 1990. (Available through USFWS.)

> Contact: U.S. Fish and Wildlife Service
> Publications Unit, Arlington Square
> 849 C Street NW
> Washington, DC 20240
> http://www.fws.gov/

Release, an exciting twenty-four-minute video documenting the first all-volunteer U.S. whale rescue, rehabilitation, and release, coordinated by two (noncaptive) marine mammal/wildlife rescue organizations.

> Contact: Marine Mammal Conservancy
> PO Box 1625
> Key Largo, FL 33037
> 305-853-0675
> www.pennekamp.com/mmc/
> E-mail: mmc@pennekamp.com

Books on Animal/Wildlife Careers

Camenson, Blythe. *Great Jobs for Biology Majors.* VGM Career Horizons, 1999.

————. *Opportunities in Zoo Careers.* VGM Career Horizons, 1998.

Collard, Sneed B., III. *A Whale Biologist at Work.* Franklin Watts, 2000.

Hamilton, John. *Eco-Careers: A Guide to Jobs in the Environmental Field.* Abdo and Daughters, 1993.

Maynard, Thane. *Working with Wildlife.* Franklin Watts, 1999.

Reeves, Diane Lindsey, and Nancy Heubeck. *Career Ideas for Kids Who Like Animals and Nature.* Checkmark Books, 2000.

Sirch, Willow Ann. *Careers with Animals.* The Humane Society of the United States, Fulcrum Resources, 2000.

Websites on Animal/Wildlife Careers

Ark Animal Tracks: good selection of books on animal careers, environmental jobs, veterinary jobs, and summer job information. www.arkanimals.com/Ecommerce/Books/careerbk.htm

National Association of Veterinary Technicians in America. www.navta.net

National Wildlife Rehabilitators Association (NWRA): Under "Careers," information on how to find jobs in wildlife rehabilitation, recommended education and qualifications needed, range of salaries, suggestions on getting beneficial experience, licensing, state and national regulations, professional standards, and related fields of study and experience. www.nwrawildlife.org

The Society for Marine Mammalogy: Strategies for Pursuing a Career in Marine Mammal Science: comprehensive information that answers commonly asked questions and provides suggestions on how to plan education and work experience. http://www.marinemammalogy.org/

U.S. Fish and Wildlife Service: "Careers: Conserving the Nature of America." hr.fws.gov/Careers_FWS.htm

Organizations Supporting Wildlife and Habitat Protection

Below are a few well-known organizations that help protect wild animals and their habitats. Check out their websites with many links to other resources.

American Bird Conservancy:
www.abcbirds.org
PO Box 249
The Plains, VA 20198
540-253-5780
E-mail: abc@abcbirds.org

Audubon Society: www.audubon.org
700 Broadway
New York, NY 10003
212-979-3000
E-mail: join@audubon.org

Bat Conservation International:
www.batcon.org
PO Box 162603
Austin, TX 78716
512-327-9721
E-mail: batinfo@batcon.org

The Cousteau Society:
www.cousteausociety.org
870 Greenbrier Circle, Suite 402
Chesapeake, VA 23320
800-441-4395
E-mail: cousteau@cousteausociety.org

Defenders of Wildlife: www.defenders.org
National Headquarters 1101
14th Street NW, #1400
Washington, DC 20005
202-682-9400
E-mail: info@defenders.org

The Fund for Animals: www.fund.org
200 W. 57th Street
New York, NY 10019
212-246-2096
E-mail: fundinfo@fund.org

Humane Society of the United States:
www.hsus.org
2100 L Street NW
Washington, DC 20037
202-452-1100
E-mail: member@hsus.org

National Wildlife Federation: www.nwf.org
11100 Wildlife Center Drive
Reston, VA 20190
800-822-9919
E-mail: info@nwf.org

The Nature Conservancy: http://nature.org
4245 N. Fairfax Drive, Suite 100
Arlington, VA 22203-1606
800-628-6860
E-mail: comment@tnc.org

Save the Manatee Club:
    www.savethemanatee.org
500 N. Maitland Avenue
Maitland, FL 32751
800-432-5646
E-mail: Education@savethemanatee.org

Sierra Club: www.sierraclub.org
85 Second Street, 2nd Floor
San Francisco, CA 94105
415-977-5500
E-mail: information@sierraclub.org

The Wilderness Society: www.wilderness.org
1615 M Street NW
Washington, DC 20036
800-843-9453
E-mail: tws@wilderness.org

World Wildlife Fund: www.worldwildlife.org
1250 24th Street NW
Washington, DC 20037
800-960-0993
E-mail: wwfus@worldwildlife.org

Learning More About Wildlife Rehabilitation

Many websites offer good information about wildlife rehabilitation. Some even include the important topics of ethics and professional standards because new rehabilitators need to learn how to care for wildlife properly, legally, and ethically.

Unfortunately, a few websites present outdated or incorrect information. Because it can be difficult for the average person to know what is accurate and what is not, a few good resources are listed in this section to help interested people get a good start gathering proper and current information about wildlife rehabilitation.

Do You Want to Become a Wildlife Rehabilitator?

The following websites are the best places to start, especially those of the two national organizations, National Wildlife Rehabilitators Association and International Wildlife Rehabilitation Council. If you do not own a computer, check with your local library about using one there. These sites offer excellent literature for purchase and materials that can be downloaded, including descriptions of what is required to become a rehabilitator, professional standards, regulations, wildlife emergencies, and how to find a rehabilitation mentor or sponsor, among others. They also provide links to other rehabilitation and wildlife organizations.

International Wildlife Rehabilitation Council
    (IWRC): www.iwrc-online.org
4437 Central Place, Suite B-4
Suisun, CA 94585-1633
707-864-1761
E-mail: iwrc@inreach.com

"Introduction to Wildlife Rehabilitation," an Internet class that helps you decide if wildlife rehab is for you:
    class.universalclass.com/chash/w/i/l/
    wildliferehab.htm
(or do a search for "Universal Class")

National Wildlife Rehabilitators Association
(NWRA): www.nwrawildlife.org
14 N. 7th Avenue
St. Cloud, MN 56303-4766
320-259-4086
E-mail: nwra@nwrawildlife.org

WildAgain Wildlife Rehabilitation, Inc.:
www.ewildagain.org
PO Box 685
Evergreen, CO 80437-0685
E-mail: ewildagn@aol.com

Wildlife International:
www.wildlife-international.org
Includes comprehensive information about
wildlife in general, a "Help" section for people
who have found hurt wildlife, and a rehabilitation section for rehabilitators looking for
current information in the field. Created and
maintained by IWRC.

The Wildlife Rehabilitation Information
Directory: www.tc.umn.edu/~devo0028/
(Search for "Wildlife Rehabilitation Information Directory" if you cannot link to the site
with the above URL.)

WildlifeRehabber.com:
www.wildliferehabber.com
Includes a Wildlife section for the public with
general wildlife information (assistance with
nuisance wildlife, what to do when finding or-
phaned/injured wildlife, etc.), a Contacts section to help people locate a rehabilitator
nearby, a Shopping section that provides links
to online sources of wildlife-oriented books and
supplies, and a Rehabilitation Database, which
is restricted to WildlifeRehabber.com members.

Training Programs

Both NWRA and IWRC hold annual conferences. They also offer several training programs
that include everything from principles of wildlife rehabilitation to physical therapy for wildlife
to volunteer management. Both organizations post information on employment in the wildlife
rehabilitation field on their websites; NWRA provides a section on internships.

In addition, state and regional wildlife rehabilitation associations offer training and conferences for new and experienced rehabilitators. Check them out at www.nwrawildlife.org/
documents/stateprovgroups.pdf.

WildAgain (www.ewildagain.org) offers a variety of seminars and training programs to help
rehabilitators, such as wildlife rehabilitation practices that include wildlife hotlines, caging, nutrition, and health care; establishing and managing nonprofit organizations; and policies and
regulations affecting wildlife. The website posts a schedule for rehabilitation conferences and
other training opportunities.

A few other organizations with good examples of informative websites are Tri-State Bird Rescue
& Research, Inc. (www.tristatebird.org), Wildlife Center of Virginia (www.wildlifecenter.org),
The Marine Mammal Center (www.tmmc.org/), PAWS (www.paws.org), and The Fund for
Animals Wildlife Rehabilitation Center (http://www.fundwildlife.org/). You can find many
more by doing an Internet search for "wildlife rehabilitation" or "wildlife rescue."

Magazines/Journals

Members of IWRC receive *Journal of Wildlife Rehabilitation* quarterly. NWRA members receive quarterly issues of *The Wildlife Rehabilitator* and biannual publications of *Wildlife Rehabilitation Bulletin*. In addition, both organizations offer publications for new and experienced rehabilitators that can be ordered via their websites.

Wildlife Rehabilitation Today, semiannual magazine: www.wildliferehabtoday.com
Coconut Creek Publishing Company
2300 W. Sample Road, Suite 314
Pompano Beach, FL 33073-3046
954-977-5058
E-mail: info@wildliferehabtoday.com

Getting Started in Wildlife Rehabilitation

Volunteering with a licensed, experienced wildlife rehabilitator or a center is the best way to start learning how to care for injured and orphaned wildlife.

An excellent resource booklet, "Wildlife Rehabilitation: Is It for You?" describes what wildlife rehabilitation is, why it's needed, different types of rehabilitation, facilities and common activities, basic requirements, common myths, ways to become a rehabilitator, and how to get started. You can download it from WildAgain Wildlife Rehabilitation, Inc., at www.ewildagain.org under the heading "Becoming a Wildlife Rehabilitator." If you do not have access to a computer, contact WildAgain at the address listed earlier in this section.

Most states require wildlife rehabilitators to be licensed in order to legally care for wildlife. Some will allow individuals to obtain permits through a licensed wildlife rehabilitation center.

Wildlife Diseases

Zoonoses are diseases that humans can get from wildlife. At least 150 zoonotic diseases are known. Among them are rabies, anthrax, Rocky Mountain spotted fever, and Lyme disease. The most recent is West Nile virus.

With good training, wildlife rehabilitators learn how to prevent contracting diseases that might be carried by wildlife. For example, those who work with animals more likely to carry rabies (foxes, coyote, skunks, raccoons, and bats) protect themselves by receiving vaccinations against rabies and getting boosters when needed.

Those who work with raccoons need to be aware of *Baylisascaris procyonis*, a raccoon roundworm that can be lethal to humans, especially small children. An adult worm can produce millions of eggs per day, and if humans accidentally ingest them, the hatched larvae can penetrate the intestines and migrate to the eyes, brain, or spinal cord. Because the eggs are very difficult to destroy, cages or carriers occupied by raccoons should not house any other species. This is why the general public should not be handling or housing raccoons—even baby animals—and children should not be around them.

Below are a few websites with information about zoonoses.

Cornell University: "What's Going on with West Nile Virus?" www.cfe.cornell.edu/erap/WNV/

National Center for Infectious Diseases: http://www.cdc.gov/ncidod/diseases/index.htm

USDA Pest Management Centers: "West Nile Virus in North America," www.ncpmc.org/
NewsAlerts/westnilevirus.html

Veterinary Support Personnel Network: "Zoonoses and Public Health": www.vspn.org/
LIBRARY/WWWDirectory/Zoonoses.htm

Wildlife Rehabilitation Information Directory: "Health Concerns to Be Aware of When Working with Wildlife," www.tc.umn.edu/~devo0028/zoonos.htm

State Wildlife Agencies

Alabama Division of Wildlife &
    Freshwater Fisheries
Department of Conservation & Natural
    Resources
64 N. Union Street
Montgomery, AL 36130
334-242-3465
www.dcnr.state.al.us/agfd/

Alaska Department of Fish & Game
PO Box 25526
Juneau, AK 99802
907-465-4100
www.state.ak.us/local/akpages/FISH.GAME/
    adfghome.htm

Arizona Game and Fish Department
2221 W. Greenway Road
Phoenix, AZ 85023
602-789-3278
www.gf.state.az.us/welcome.html

Arkansas Game & Fish Commission
2 Natural Resources Drive
Little Rock, AR 72205
501-223-6305
www.agfc.state.ar.us/

California Department of Fish & Game
PO Box 944209
Sacramento, CA 94244
916-653-7667
www.dfg.ca.gov/

Colorado Division of Wildlife
6060 Broadway
Denver, CO 80216-1000
303-291-7208
www.wildlife.state.co.us/

Connecticut Department of
    Environmental Protection
79 Elm Street
Hartford, CT 06106
860-424-3010
www.dep.state.ct.us/

Delaware Division of Fish and Wildlife
89 Kings Highway
Dover, DE 19901
302-739-5295
www.dnrec.state.de.us/

Florida Fish & Wildlife
    Conservation Commission
620 S. Meridian Street
Tallahassee, FL 32399-1600
850-488-2975
www.fcn.state.fl.us/gfc/home.html

Georgia Wildlife Resources Division
Special Permit Unit
2070 U.S. Highway 278 SE
Social Circle, GA 30025
770-918-6401
www.dnr.state.ga.us/

Hawaii Department of Land &
   Natural Resources
PO Box 621
Honolulu, HI 96809
808-587-0400
www.state.hi.us/dlnr

Idaho Fish & Game Department
600 S. Walnut Street
PO Box 25
Boise, ID 83707-0025
208-334-5159
www2.state.id.us/fishgame/

Illinois Department of Natural Resources
524 S. Second Street
Springfield, IL 62701-1787
217-785-0075
dnr.state.il.us/

Indiana Division of Fish and Wildlife
402 W. Washington Street
Room W-273
Indianapolis, IN 46204
317-232-4080
www.state.in.us/dnr/fishwild/index.htm

Iowa Department of Natural Resources
East Ninth and Grand Avenue
Des Moines, IA 50319-0034
515-281-5385
www.state.ia.us/government/dnr/index.htm

Kansas Department of Wildlife and Parks
900 SW Jackson, Suite 502
Topeka, KS 66612-1233
785-296-2281
www.kdwp.state.ks.us/

Kentucky Department of Fish &
   Wildlife Resources
1 Game Farm Road
Frankfort, KY 40601
502-564-3400
www.state.ky.us/agencies/fw/kdfwr.htm

Louisiana Department of
   Wildlife & Fisheries
PO Box 98000
Baton Rouge, LA 70898-9000
225-765-2623
www.wlf.state.la.us/

Maine Department of Inland
   Fisheries & Wildlife
284 State Street, Station 41
Augusta, ME 04333
207-287-5202
www.state.me.us/ifw/homepage.htm

Maryland Department of Natural Resources
Wildlife Division
Tawes State Office Building
Annapolis, MD 21401
410-260-8281
www.dnr.state.md.us/

Massachusetts Department of Fisheries,
   Wildlife, and Environmental
   Law Enforcement
1 Rabbit Hill Road
Westborough, MA 01581
508-792-7270
www.state.ma.us/dfwele/dfw

Michigan Department of Natural Resources
PO Box 30028
Lansing, MI 48909-7944
517-373-2329
www.michigan.gov/dnr

Minnesota Division of Wildlife
Department of Natural Resources
500 Lafayette Road
St. Paul, MN 55155-4007
651-297-4960
www.dnr.state.mn.us/

Mississippi Department of Wildlife,
   Fisheries & Parks
1505 Eastover Drive
Jackson, MS 39211-6374
601-432-2400
www.mdwfp.com/

Missouri Department of Conservation
PO Box 180
Jefferson City, MO 65102-0180
573-751-4115
www.conservation.state.mo.us/

Montana Department of Fish, Wildlife,
    and Parks
PO Box 200701
Helena, MT 59620
406-4443186
www.fwp.state.mt.us

Nebraska Game and Parks Commission
2200 N. 33rd, PO Box 30370
Lincoln, NE 68510
402-471-5539
www.ngpc.state.ne.us/homepage.html

Nevada Division of Wildlife
1100 Valley Road, PO Box 10678
Reno, NV 89512
775-688-1599
www.nevadadivisionofwildlife.org

New Hampshire Fish and Game Department
2 Hazen Drive
Concord, NH 03301
603-271-3422
www.wildlife.state.nh.us/

New Jersey Division of Fish & Wildlife
PO Box 400
Trenton, NJ 08625
609-292-9410
www.state.nj.us/dep/fgw/

New Mexico Game & Fish Department
1 Wildlife Way
Santa Fe, NM 87507
505-476-8008
www.gmfsh.state.nm.us/

New York Division of Fish, Wildlife, &
    Marine Resources
Department of Environmental Conservation
625 Broadway, 5th Floor
Albany, NY 12233
518-402-8924
www.dec.state.ny.us/

North Carolina Wildlife
    Resources Commission
512 N. Salisbury Street
Raleigh, NC 27604
919-733-3391
www.ncwildlife.org

North Dakota Game & Fish Department
100 North Bismarck Expressway
Bismarck, ND 58501
701-328-6300
www.state.nd.us/gnf/

Ohio Division of Wildlife
1840 Belcher Drive
Columbus, OH 43224-1329
614-265-6300
www.dnr.state.oh.us/wildlife/default.htm

Oklahoma Department of
    Wildlife Conservation
1801 N. Lincoln Boulevard
Oklahoma City, OK 73105
405-521-3851
www.state.ok.us/~odwc/

Oregon Department of Fish & Wildlife
2501 SW First Avenue, PO Box 59
Portland, OR 97207
503-872-5310
www.dfw.state.or.us/

Pennsylvania Game Commission
2001 Elmerton Avenue
Harrisburg, PA 17110-9797
717-787-3633
www.pgc.state.pa.us/

Rhode Island Division of Fish & Wildlife
4808 Tower Hill Road
Wakefield, RI 02879
401-789-3094
www.state.ri.us/dem/programs/bnatres/
    fishwild/index.htm

South Carolina Department of
    Natural Resources
PO Box 167
Columbia, SC 29202
803-734-6310
www.dnr.state.sc.us/

South Dakota Game, Fish, &
Parks Department
523 E. Capitol
Pierre, SD 57501-3182
605-773-3387
www.state.sd.us/gfp/

Tennessee Wildlife Resources
PO Box 40747
Nashville, TN 37204-9979
615-781-6552
www.state.tn.us/twra/index.html

Texas Parks and Wildlife Department
4200 Smith School Road
Austin, TX 78744
512-389-4814
www.tpwd.state.tx.us/

Utah Division of Wildlife Resources
1594 W. North Temple, Suite 2110
PO Box 146301
Salt Lake City, UT 84114
801-538-4703
www.nr.state.ut.us/dwr/dwr.htm

Vermont Department of Fish & Wildlife
103 S. Main Street, Suite 10 South
Waterbury, VT 05671-0501
802-241-3730
www.anr.state.vt.us/fw/fwhome/index.htm

Virginia Department of Game &
Inland Fisheries
PO Box 11104
4010 W. Broad Street
Richmond, VA 23230-1104
804-367-9231
www.dgif.state.va.us/

Washington Department of Fish
and Wildlife
600 Capital Way North
Olympia, WA 98501-1091
360-902-2225
www.wa.gov/wdfw/

West Virginia Division of Natural Resources
Wildlife Resources Section
1900 Kanawha Boulevard East
Charleston, WV 25305
304-558-2771
www.dnr.state.wv.us/

Wisconsin Department of Natural Resources
PO Box 7921
Madison, WI 53707-7921
608-266-2121
www.dnr.state.wi.us/

Wyoming Game and Fish Department
3400 Bishop Boulevard
Cheyenne, WY 82006
307-777-4600
gf.state.wy.us/

U.S. Fish and Wildlife Service Regional Offices

Contact this government service about migratory birds or endangered species.

Region 1—Pacific (California, Hawaii, Idaho, Nevada, Oregon, Washington)
U.S. Fish and Wildlife Service
911 NE 11th Avenue
Portland, OR 97232
503-231-6118
pacific.fws.gov/

Region 2—Southwest (Arizona, New Mexico, Oklahoma, Texas)
U.S. Fish and Wildlife Service
PO Box 1306
Albuquerque, NM 87103
505-248-6911
southwest.fws.gov/

Region 3—Great Lakes–Big Rivers (Illinois, Indiana, Iowa, Michigan, Minnesota, Missouri, Ohio, Wisconsin)
U.S. Fish and Wildlife Service
Federal Building
1 Federal Drive
Fort Snelling, MN 55111-4056
612-713-5301
greatlakes.fws.gov/

Region 4—Southeast (Alabama, Arkansas, Florida, Georgia, Kentucky, Louisiana, Mississippi, North Carolina, South Carolina, Tennessee)
U.S. Fish and Wildlife Service
1875 Century Boulevard
Atlanta, GA 30345
404-679-4000
southeast.fws.gov/

Region 5—Northeast (Connecticut, D.C., Delaware, Maine, Maryland, Massachusetts, New Hampshire, New Jersey, New York, Pennsylvania, Rhode Island, Vermont, Virginia, West Virginia)
U.S. Fish and Wildlife Service
300 Westgate Center Drive
Hadley, MA 01035
413-253-8200
northeast.fws.gov/

Region 6—Mountain-Prairie (Colorado, Kansas, Montana, Nebraska, North Dakota, South Dakota, Utah, Wyoming)
U.S. Fish and Wildlife Service
PO Box 25486
Denver, CO 80025
303-236-7920
mountain-prairie.fws.gov/

Region 7—Alaska
U.S. Fish and Wildlife Service
1011 E. Tudor Road
Anchorage, AK 99503
907-786-3309
alaska.fws.gov/

The Artists

Contributing Illustrators

Donna Clement (Longmont, Colorado) has volunteered at Birds of Prey Foundation in Broomfield, Colorado, for many years. She has been involved in many aspects of BOP, including giving injured raptors a ride to the foundation when called on. Clement is at her best providing beautiful pen-and-ink illustrations of Colorado's birds of prey. BOP has used Donna's artwork on T-shirts, brochures, and in educational materials. Donna also designs and paints sets for a local theater and does a variety of freelance work, including theatrical murals, illustrations, and portraits in the Denver-Boulder area.

David McCoy (east Tennessee) was a building designer, specializing in custom homes. He died in 1998. A member of the American Institute of Building Design, McCoy used his skills to design and build flight cages for his wife (and rehabilitator), Lynne. He was also a wildlife artist as well as his wife's "right hand" in support of wildlife work.

Paula Nicholas (Denver, Colorado) has worked many years as a scientific illustrator, completing biological, botanical, environmental, and medical artwork for various purposes. Originally from southern California, she has lived and worked in Colorado since 1977. Nicholas has a broad educational background in science and earned her M.S. from Colorado State University in Fort Collins. She also has had many other varied work experiences, including environmental consulting, scientific researcher, grant writer, and science and illustration teacher positions.

Contributing Photographers

Susan Ahalt (Cody, Wyoming) is director of Ironside Bird Rescue.

Luanne Albright (Epping, New Hampshire) is a wildlife rehabilitator licensed in the state of New Hampshire, specializing in bats.

Stanley B. Ashbrook (Largo, Florida) has been a dedicated amateur nature photographer for over forty years. His photos have appeared in newspapers, books, and magazines, including *National Wildlife* and *Guidepost*.

Ken Bach (San Raton, California) has been with The Marine Mammal Center in Sausalito, California, for several years. Photography and animals have been part of his life since he started an animal shelter in 1975 and was the photo editor for his high school yearbook in 1977.

Caroline Brawner (Cape Town, South Africa) volunteered at The Marine Mammal Center in Sausalito, California, from 1984 to 1986.

Shannon Brink (Denver, Colorado), age sixteen, enjoys photography, soccer, and reading.

Helen Connor (Tuscaloosa, Alabama), a professor emeritus at the University of Alabama, was a volunteer with Alabama Wildlife Rehabilitation Center and a librarian, among other varied activities (1986–1991).

Gary Crandall (Salt Lake City, Utah) has owned and operated Dancing Crane Productions (www.DancingCrane.com) since 1991. It features his hauntingly beautiful wildlife photography, which depicts animals in their natural habitats, undisturbed. None of the wildlife has been rented, baited, or harassed in any way. The cover photo he shot for this book is the first time Crandall has included people with wildlife.

Greg Crenshaw was a volunteer for Alabama Wildlife Rehabilitation Center for three years, while living in Birmingham. He enjoyed any opportunity to capture wild patients on film. Crenshaw now lives in northwest Alabama, where he opened a studio for children's portraiture. He's now able to photograph wild creatures on a daily basis. He also continues to volunteer in the Shoals area.

Critter Alley (see Janet Walker)

Coleen Doucette (Newark, Delaware) is a veterinary technician and wildlife rehabilitator working with Tri-State Bird Rescue and Research.

Greg Ewert (Lopez Island, Washington) is a teacher on Lopez Island. He photographed the beautiful and inspiring book *Kindred Spirits: Stories, Passions, and Portraits from the Heart of Community*.

Rosa and Dave Felder live in Broomfield, Colorado.

Tom Fell lives in Cody, Wyoming.

John Findlay III became known as "Mr. Bluebird" after starting a Bluebird Trail in Oak Mountain State Park (Alabama) in 1979. From seven boxes it expanded into 180 boxes, 100 of which were in the park and the others in Jefferson and Shelby Counties. Findlay was born and grew up in Wakefield, Massachusetts. He lived in Illinois for twenty-eight years and in Birmingham, Alabama, for eighteen. Because of Findlay's work with bluebirds in the park, the main road was named the John Findlay III Road. He died in 1995.

Doug Franklin is an artist who lives in western Colorado.

Kari Gabriel lives in Kalispell, Montana.

Bobbi J. Geise is director of Bridger Outdoor Science School in Bozeman, Montana. Formerly she was director of Big Sky Wildcare, a raptor rehabilitation facility.

Greenwood Wildlife Rehabilitation Sanctuary, PO Box 18987, Boulder, CO 80308, 303-545-5849.

Kim Heacox (Gustavus, Alaska) has written and photographed several books on Alaska, including *In Denali* and *Alaska Light*.

Harvey and Pamela Hergett (Quincy, California) were volunteers at Alaska Raptor Center from 1993 to 1996.

Catherine Hurlbutt (Denver, Colorado) has loved birds all of her ninety years. A government stenographer for forty-one years, Hurlbutt has also rescued and rehabilitated birds for many decades. She has written nine remarkable books about her experiences with birds.

George Jackson (Denver, Colorado) is an executive search consultant with a passion for motorcycles. He and his wife, Shannon Jacobs, enjoy traveling and photographing wildlife.

Diane Johnson (Linwood, Kansas) is a licensed veterinary technician who has worked for area veterinarians for more than twenty years. She is founder and director of Operation WildLife (OWL), the largest wildlife rehabilitation center in the state of Kansas.

Michael Judish (Northglenn, Colorado) has taken stunning photographs of weather phenomena, dynamic landscapes, and wildlife for many years.

Amanda Lollar (Mineral Wells, Texas) is the author of *The Bat in My Pocket* and coauthor of *Captive Care and Medical Reference for the Rehabilitation of Insectivorous Bats*. She's also a scientific wildlife rehabilitator and the director of Bat World Sanctuary in Mineral Wells.

Sally Maughan (Boise, Idaho) is the founder of Coyote Foster Parent Program and Idaho Black Bear Rehab, Inc.

Lynne McCoy (east Tennessee) has been a wildlife rehabilitator for more than twenty-five years. She uses a Minolta Freedom Zoom camera and relies on 400-speed film and the trusty camera. "If I tried to manage f-stops, etc., my critters would be long gone!" she says. So she tries to "quick catch" personalities of her patients on film.

Jane Oka (Mill Valley, California) is a graphic designer and illustrator in the real world, but she cannot envision life without the rich experience and privileges of working in close proximity to wildlife. Photography is Oka's creative extension at The Marine Mammal Center in Sausalito, California. Her participation in animal care began in 1979. She's been shift supervisor since 1983.

Rosemary Perfit lives in Tampa, Florida.

Phylis Rollins (Dandridge, Tennessee) spent many years in the San Francisco Bay area rehabilitating wildlife and animals most people find boring—turtles, opossums, skunks—and discovered that the sweetest, most fascinating teachers in life are quite often those overlooked. She moved to the woodlands of east Tennessee to live a simpler lifestyle devoted to the land and wildlife. Besides rehabilitating, Rollins enjoys meditation, writing, and native crafts.

Cindy Rork (Denver, Colorado) is an elementary school teacher. She does several wildlife rescue projects with her students each year. Rork has twin sons, Andrew and Chris.

Tom Sanders and his wife, Cec (Florence, Colorado), have been married thirty years and have been wildlife rehabilitators for nearly all their married life. They operate Wet Mountain Wildlife Rehabilitation, a facility for helping the wildlife of Colorado.

Chris Schulz (Castle Hayne, North Carolina) is a volunteer with the Marine Mammal Conservancy in Key Largo and Wildlife Rescue of the Florida Keys. She's also a member of the Florida Keys Marine Mammal Rescue Team.

Wendy Shattil and Bob Rozinski (Denver, Colorado) are widely published professional nature and wildlife photographers noted for their behavioral and evocative images.

Paula Stolebarger lives and works in Denver, Colorado.

Amy Sweeney (Sitka, Alaska) is a volunteer and supporter of Alaska Raptor Center. She has a home-based business, Sand Dollar Designs. Her specialty is northern lights photography, but she also does specialty printing, illustrations, and graphic design.

Texas State Aquarium, 2710 N. Shoreline Boulevard, Corpus Christi, TX 78402, 800-477-GULF.

Sigrid Ueblacker (Broomfield, Colorado) is the founder and director of Birds of Prey Foundation.

Urban Wildlife Rescue (Denver, Colorado) was formed by Jack and Penny Murphy in November 1991. They rehabilitate 150 to 200 fur-bearing mammals annually. The animals range from bats to coyotes. The Murphys give 75 to 100 educational programs every year to schools, animal control agencies, and homeowner associations. Through Urban Wildlife Rescue's "Humane Solutions to Wildlife Problems," 3,000 citizens are helped with wildlife conflicts annually, either over the phone or with on-site assistance. More than 8,000 wild animals are saved each year because of this program.

Karen Von den Deale (Brewster, Massachusetts) has been a state and federally licensed wildlife rehabilitator since 1989. She founded Wild Care, Inc., in 1994, when an "empty nest syndrome" led her back to her childhood love of nature—the wild outdoors and animals. Wild Care admits about 1,400 birds, mammals, and reptiles annually, and the animals are treated with the highest professional standards. Von den Deale remains an amateur photographer.

Janet Walker (Grand Ledge, Michigan) is a state and federally licensed wildlife rehabilitator who has rehabilitated wildlife for over twenty-five years. She was the executive director of Critter Alley Wildlife Rehabilitation Center, one of the nation's largest and most comprehensive rehab centers.

B. D. Wehrfritz (Meeteetse, Wyoming) is a professional wildlife nature photographer who volunteers photographic services for Ironside Bird Rescue in Cody, Wyoming.

W.E.R.C.: Wildlife Education and Rehabilitation Center, PO Box 1105, Morgan Hill, CA 95038, (408) 779-WERC.

Index

Horn, Laurel: photo of, 145
Hospitals, 55, 88–91; avian, 111; wildlife, 24
Hot Pepper repellent, recipe for, 179
"House on My Back" (Wild Care), 116
Housing, ix, 3, 8
Howell, Sue: Helmethead and, 57
"How to Make Your Outdoor Cat a Happy Indoor
   Cat" (Winter), 126, 127–28
Huckabee, John R., 4, 5; photo of, 4; Three L's
   and, 142
Hughes, Joan: gulls and, 29
Humane societies, 17
Humane solutions, 21, 149–50
Human scent, 20
Hummingbirds, 103; photo of, 103; planting for,
   138, 138 (photo)
Humpback whales, 85–86; photo of, 86
Humphrey (humpback whale), 85–86; photo of, 86
Humpty Dumpty (turtle), story of, 73–74
Hunting, responsible, 129–30
Hurlbutt, Catherine (Birdie), 21; photo of, 21
Hydroelectric plants, 89
Hypothermia, 89, 91

I

Idaho Black Bear Rehab, Inc., 25
Imprinting, 34–35, 52, 188
Incubators, 24, 25, 188; photo of, 33
Injuries, ix–x, 3, 136, 157–61; internal, 24;
   preventing, ix, 48, 49; rehabilitating, 150, 151;
   serious, 24, 46, 48
Instincts, 188; defense/survival, 136, 152; dog/cat,
   136
International Bird Rescue Research Center, 59
International Wildlife Rehabilitation Council
   (IWRC), 9
Ironside Bird Rescue, 41, 43, 51
It's a Wildlife (newsletter), 64
IWRC. See International Wildlife Rehabilitation
   Council

J

Jake the Entertainer (opossum), 65; photo of, 65
Jambo (California sea otter), 87; photo of, 87
Jaws (opossum), photo of, 6
Jellyfish, 132
Jesses, 53, 188
Johnson, Diane, 53, 134, 135; photo of, 53
Judish, Michael: raptor rescue and, 12
July, Mark: photo of, 49
Junior Volunteer Program, 76

K

Kandi (pilot whale), 96, 98–99; photo of, 99
Kavookjian, Peggy, 15
Kemp's ridley sea turtles, 92, 93; photo of, 93
Kestrels, photo of, 41

Kidnapping, 13–14, 25, 34, 39, 49, 133–36;
   preventing, 152
"Kids and Critters Club," 95
Kimball, Terry: photo of, 77
KimBEARly (bear cub), photo of, 41
Kingbirds, photo of, 27
Kingfishers, feeding, 30 (photo)
Kinky (squirrel), photo of, 74

L

Lake Okeechobee, 90
Landing craft, photo of, 98
Leash-training, 128
Lee, Ken: photo of, 86
Letters of Authorization (LOA), 7
Liberty Wildlife Rehabilitation Foundation, 15, 34,
   53
Lice, 16, 19
Lingenfelser, Robert: photo of, 97
Lisle, Jean: photo of, 17
Litter, cleaning up, 131–32
Living With Deer, website of, 168
LOA. See Letters of Authorization
Locks, 90, 188
Lollar, Amanda, 55; Bat Chats and, 70; Bat World
   and, 68, 148; on Bucko, 71; Enchanted Forest
   and, 69; photo of, 68; rehabilitation by, 69
Lowry Park Zoo, 89; manatees at, 55, 88, 91; photo
   of, 33, 88, 90
Lucky Frank (manatee), 91; photo of, 91

M

Mack, Kevin: photo of, 4
Maggots, 73, 76, 189
Magical Skunk Deodorizer, recipe for, 178
Malnutrition, 30, 67
Manatee and Aquatic Center, 89
Manatee Hospital, 55
Manatees: caring for, 88–91; food for, 90; mystery
   disease for, 88–89; photo of, 33, 88, 89, 90, 91;
   post-release studies on, 55–56
Mange, 134, 189; photo of, 134
Manning, 53, 189
Marine animals, 39, 132; cages for, 27; oil spills
   and, 58; rehabilitating, 5, 82, 83, 161
Marine Mammal Center, The (TMMC), 59, 82,
   84–87; photo of, 39, 84; volunteers from, 11
   (photo), 45 (photo)
Marine Mammal Conservancy (MMC), 81, 83, 96
Marine Mammal Health and Stranding Response
   Program, 100
Marine Patrol, 17, 99
Mariner Resort, 98
Marmots, hibernation by, 62
Marsupials, 6, 189
Maughan, Sally, 25, 26
Maynard (cormorant), 110, 111